ZODIAC

WEST SUSSEX

Edited by Steve Twelvetree

First published in Great Britain in 2002 by
YOUNG WRITERS
Remus House,
Coltsfoot Drive,
Peterborough, PE2 9JX
Telephone (01733) 890066

HB ISBN 0 75433 520 8
SB ISBN 0 75433 521 6

FOREWORD

Young Writers was established in 1991 with the aim of promoting creative writing in children, to make reading and writing poetry fun.

Once again, this year proved to be a tremendous success with over 41,000 entries received nationwide.

The Zodiac competition has shown us the high standard of work and effort that children are capable of today. The competition has given us a vivid insight into the thoughts and experiences of today's younger generation. It is a reflection of the enthusiasm and creativity that teachers have injected into their pupils, and it shines clearly within this anthology.

The task of selecting poems was a difficult one, but nevertheless, an enjoyable experience. We hope you are as pleased with the final selection in *Zodiac West Sussex* as we are.

CONTENTS

Michelle Barnett	68
Mark Maskell	68
Leena Patel	69
Tracey Woolford	69
Naomi West	70
Joanne Chapman	70
Daniel Kania	71
Stephen Weston	71
Chris Kizza	71
Joanne Nash	72
Nicola Wenham	72
Ros February	72
Nasima Kada	73
Rebecca Jones	74
Joanne Pullen	75
Emma Barling	76
Jonathan Baldry	77
Charlotte Walker	78
Elaine Willoughby	79
Charlotte Ellis	80

Littlegreen School

Leszek Ujma	81
Karl Day	82
James Gatfield	82
Ryan Breach	83
Shane Marshall	84
Wayne Edwards	84
Tom Stevens	85
Matt Batchelor	86

Millais School For Girls

Amélie Desbiens	87
Rosanna Morgan	88
Claire Allen	89
Tamsin Davison	90
Julia Rose	91
Nicola Titterrell	92

Oakmeeds Community College

Sally-Ann Hill	93
Helen Ahier	93
Michael Poole	94
Claire Ellis	94
Stephanie Combe	95
Hannah Lathwell	96
Aled Hancock	96
Sammy Jolley	96
Claire Mallows	97
Daniel Beard	97
Hannah Riddleston	98
Thomas Grimes	98
Charlotte Woodward	98
Jessica Zmak	99
Jacqui Taylor	99
Jamie Hillwood	100
Timmy Gedin	100
Meggie Whaley	101
Anna Harper	102
Natalia James	102
Nicola Ridley	103
James Keates	103
Ben Ingram	104
Jason Dela Nougerede	104
Victoria Riddleston	105
Siobhan Hancock	105
Grace Hill	106
Joshua Reeve	106
Hannah Denyer	107
Devon Busby	107
Stephanie Brown	108
Tom Whitworth	108
Laura Jupp	109
Tim Cooper	110

The Poems

THE FATE OF THE WESTERN WORLD

I see the future, what will be, I can see
Your life, their life and our life.
I see good and bad, right and wrong, love and hate.
People's fate in my hands.
It is written in the stars, your life, their life and our life.
Will our lives last forever, do we love another,
Shall we answer our deepest questions? If yes,
Who will do it for us?
Flying high above the world, people with you, innocent
Alone, unaware of the path that lies ahead of them.
I see pain and suffering, hatred, anger and revenge.
Politics shall rule our world, but not others.
Is your life controllable, can you see your fate?
No, only I can see your fate.
Your stars can see your fate, but cannot tell you.
Birds of metal shall stop you, other worlds will
Help, people will stand beside you,
Afraid of what has come upon them.
Your life is on other hands, your loved ones in your own,
Settle all your arguments; make all your troubles gone.
Let all your loved ones love you, your enemies love you too,
Your friends must treasure your friendship.
Other worlds will try to rule you, but you will prevail.
People will lose lives, ready or not.
Will you be one of those great losers, will your family
Lose the greatest part of their lives, will you
Have another chance in this world of ours?
You don't know, I know. I can tell you, but will I?

Katy Crabb (12)
Angmering School

ZODIAC

Zodiac is a prediction of the sky.
If you are a Virgo, you're diligent and shy,
You explore in great details,
You have to look twice at a black cat's tail.
If you are a Libra, you're charming and urbane
And all your friends think you are very hard to tame.
If you are a Scorpio beware of the sing,
You are hanging really high from a really thin string.
If you are Sagittarius, you seek eternal joy,
You are as much fun as an excited little boy.
If you are a Capricorn, you are patient and practical,
All your family think you are really quite tactical.
If you are an Aquarius, you're honest and loyal,
You are shiny, just like tin foil.
If you are a Pisces, you are sensitive and kind,
You would kick a bully up the behind!
If you are an Aries, you are confident and quick,
You would give a lolly quite a big lick.
If you are a Taurus, you are patient and placid,
Make sure you don't touch any acid.
If you are a Gemini, you are youthful and witty,
You will grow to be really pretty.
If you are a Cancer, you are shrewd and protective,
When you are older you will be selective.
If you are a Leo, you're loving and faithful,
You will always be very tasteful.
So this is the end of the zodiac rhyme,
Please read this again another time.

Siân Collinge (12)
Angmering School

ZODIAC

My star sign is Libra
And it says I am charming and urbane.
Librans can talk their way out of any woe,
But I don't think this is at all true.
I am more like a Sagittarius,
Not actually intellectual and fun, but I seek eternal joy.
I love having fun and enjoying my spare time,
I love going out with my friends all the time.
How can fate decide my tomorrow,
Or anyone else?
Will it know what I will do tomorrow,
Will it know what I will do next?
Has it already predicted the rest of my day,
Has it predicted my next week?
How does fate know
And why can't I know what is going to happen in my life?
Everyone has a star sign,
But does it apply to everyone?
Does everybody think theirs' is true?
I know mine is not, because I am more like a Sagittarius.
Is everyone more like another sign?
I am sure there are people that think the same,
But there's probably not.
Some people probably believe in it,
Some of them are probably quite true,
Some people might think they may apply for more than one,
But that is how it is,
Everyone has their sign and that is what it is.

Abi Smith (12)
Angmering School

THE ZODIAC - CREATURES OF FATE

Aquarius, upright and devoted
A peaceful life of honesty.
Pisces, easily hurt and considerate
A day-care job for thee.

Aries, self-assured and speedy
A life of fun and games you'll try.
Taurus, tranquil and enduring
There's more to her than meets the eye.

Gemini, immature and funny
A job with children, an entertainer will do.
Cancer, clever and watchful,
He will always look after you.

Leo, reliable and warm-hearted
Is loyal to one only.
Virgo, careful and timid
Will maybe always be lonely.

Libra, charming and urbane
Will date many but maybe never settle down.
Scorpio, passionate and forceful
Many children of hers could be found.

Sagittarius, intelligent and fun
The job you'll get? Just wait and see.
Capricorn, peaceful and patient
Could be a bank accountant maybe.

Natalie McPhillips (12)
Angmering School

The Perfect Zodiac

Am I a perfect Zodiac man?
A caring, loving and honest
Person named Dan,
An Aquarius birthday date,
But will this continue to be my fate,
As I am also a sensitive type,
Perhaps like Pisces.
But then again the stars of
Aries and Taurus are both
Confident and placid,
And if by magic
I become both of these
And make friends like a youthful Gemini,
But my wit is protected by Cancer.
Like my faithful friend Leo
I am both diligent and true.
Although shy, we explore our destinies
Like true Virgos.
In times of trouble, I snow no woe
Just like my pet Libra who is not
As quick as a zebra.
With great force and power
I am able to sing my enemies
But also use intellect to achieve great glories.
Yes a Sagittarian as well, who seeks
A lot of fun on my island of Capricorn.
I am a perfect Zodiac man.

Mark Emerton (13)
Angmering School

CAPRICORN VS SAGITTARIUS

22nd December,
Border-line between Sagittarius and Capricorn.
I am supposed to be a Capricorn,
But I'm nothing like it at all.
I'm not very practical or patient,
In fact, I'm nothing like it.
I'm more of a Sagittarius,
Because I'm funny
And seek eternal joy.
Perhaps I should be called Sagicorn?

Simon Dyson (11)
Angmering School

FATE IS US

Fate brought us here,
Fate created us,
Fate *is* us.

Fate guided us,
Fate chose for us,
Fate *is* us.

Fate destroyed us,
Fate ended us,
Fate *was* us.

Chris Dingle (12)
Angmering School

NEW YORK TERROR

Shocking disturbance
The terror of New York,
The crashing of aeroplanes,
Millions of people died,
'Why?' so many people cried,
people stuck in rubble,
who is to blame?
Eight years this had been planned,
This dreadful day.
People jumping from great heights,
Firemen stuck underneath.
Suddenly it goes all quiet,
An eerie silence falls on New York.

Michael Parsons (12)
Angmering School

ZODIAC

What does the future hold?
Nobody knows.
Sometimes you just wonder about what it will be,
You could be a scientist or a builder or a dancer,
But still you don't know
What the future holds.

Samantha Stemp (12)
Angmering School

ZODIACS, HOROSCOPES

Z   is for Zodiac,
O   is for Orion,
D   is for Destiny,
I   is for Illustrated sky,
A   is for Aquarius,
C   is for Capricorn,
S   is for Stars.

H   is for Horoscopes,
O   is or Orbit,
R   is for Really amazing,
O   is for Oh so accurate,
S   is for Sagittarius,
C   is for Constellations,
O   is for Observing the planets,
P   is for Pisces,
E   is for Eclipse,
S   is for Scorpio's scorpion.

Jade Elvy (12)
Angmering School

ZODIAC

Zigzagging up and down, my brain was churning,
Oh what a terrible vision.
Do I tell anyone, or keep it to myself?
In desperation I told the world
And made a fool of myself.
Can't you see you'll be the fools in World War III?

Michael Bridges (12)
Angmering School

AM I A TYPICAL CANCER?

Am I a typical Cancer?
In terms of shrewdness
I have common sense
And I'm quite clever
But so bad at judgement.

Am I a typical Cancer?
Am I protective?
Yes, I am,
I do not run away.

Am I a typical Cancer?
Do I risk everything for love?
For love of family and friends, yes,
But no for passion.

Lewis Miller-Davey (11)
Angmering School

FATE

If fate is true,
Then why do you worry about things?
Because if everything is fate,
Then you can't do anything to change it.
So if your fate is to die,
Then there is nothing you can do.
There is no need to worry about
Something that might happen,
Because if it is fate for it to happen,
Then it will.

Martin Brown (12)
Angmering School

THE STARS

I look at the stars
To see how people are,
I study them night and day.
The signs of the zodiac
Tell me what will happen
Every start of a new day.

I have seen the past and the future,
It told me what would happen today,
But now I look at the new future,
The things that will happen on a different day.

I look at the stars
To see how people are,
I study them night and day.

Tom Newson (12)
Angmering School

AM I A TYPICAL AQUARIUS?

I am honest
And I am loyal,
I stick by my friends
And I tell the truth.

I like to see things
For myself, before
Believing someone else.
I think I'm an Aquarius.

James Millett (11)
Angmering School

ZODIAC

31st of March.
I am a confident Aries,
I may be quick, but I'm not thick.
I like to be fun and I'm hardly ever glum.
Are you Capricorn?
If you are, are you practical just like me?
Are you Aquarius?
If you are, are you honest just like me?
Are you Pisces?
If you are, are you sensitive just like me?
Are you Aries?
If you are, are you confident and quick just like me?
Are you Taurus?
If you are, are you patient just like me?
Are you?

Ashley Brett (11)
Angmering School

AMERICA

A is for Aquarius, honest and loyal,
M is for mountains of rubble,
E is for the enemy doing evil things,
R is for remembering the dead,
I   is for idiots blowing up buildings,
C is for Cancer, shrewd and protective,
A   is for American, honest and loyal.

Roxanne Street (13)
Angmering School

IT WAS MEANT TO BE

Fate - it was meant to happen,
It was meant to be that way,
The way we were all put together.

It was fate
When we were born,
It was fate.

All of our lives were put together
By the natural beings of the zodiac.
They formed us when we were born.

They all mixed together like father and mother
And from this, they planned and
Wrote our lives in the stars.

Me writing this poem, it was fate.
So can people predict the future from the stars?
The only real people who can predict the future
Are the people of the zodiac,
Not psychics or mortals,
Just the spirits that roam around in the sky.

James Flain (13)
Angmering School

ZODIAC

Cancer with its protective claws,
Leo with its faithful jaws,
Taurus with all its might,
Let fate decide my life.

Gemini with its persuasive mind,
Pisces, sensitive and kind,
Virgo, diligent and shy,
I view life through an original eye.

Aries has life wrapped in its palm,
Taurus is patient, protective and calm,
Cancer will leave nothing to win your love,
Should we be controlled by the stars above?

Christopher Hopkins (11)
Angmering School

I AM A TAURUS AND THIS IS MY HOROSCOPE!

I am a Taurus,
I am tranquil and calm
And offer safety to all I know,
This is my horoscope.

I am a Taurus,
I am loving
And hot-headed.
This is my horoscope.

I am a Taurus,
I am a hard-worker
And have feelings for all I know.
This is my horoscope.

I am a Taurus,
I am out-going
And loud.
This is my horoscope.

I am a Taurus,
I am stylish
And glamorous.
This is my horoscope.

Hazel Willis (12)
Angmering School

CAPRICORN

I take time to plan
My exciting life.
It takes me a week
To plan a day.

Am I a patient person?
Well, we will have to see.
I like to wait to see what comes
And when it comes, I take my time.
I am able to do things very easily.

So am I practical?
I can solve easy questions
Without using my head.
Yes, I'm a typical Capricorn,
But are you? We shall see.

Daniel Williams (11)
Angmering School

ZODIAC

Zodiac sounds like an alien I suppose,
Like one of those things with four green toes,
But really it's not,
It's rather quite hot
As people read them a lot.

They read them to see what the stars will say,
So they can predict the rest of the day.
True or false, you can choose,
Read them or not, there is nothing to lose.

Nichola Shaw (11)
Angmering School

ZODIAC

We are all part of the zodiac,
Some people don't want to be
But we all are.
You have no control in the zodiac.
How does this work
For every single person in the world?
We are all different and we have four lines to read.
So how does this work?

I see the future, what will you be
And who will you be with, love and hate?
I also see when you die and when you survive.

Amy Watson (12)
Angmering School

IS IT FATE?

When you peer up at the starry sky,
Do you see any writing?
Is it written up there somewhere,
Or is it just fate?

Some people think that horoscopes are true,
Others think they are not true.
Is there any proof to show that all those people
Were going to die on Tuesday, 11th September?
Was it written up there somewhere,
Or was it just fate?

Alex Price (13)
Angmering School

ZODIAC

Well, today,
I'm probably a typical Leo.
I feel faithful
And I've been loving,
Also encouraging.
I will not do this any other day,
I don't know why.
Probably I lie.
Well really,
Every other day.
I'm quite nice,
But really
I'm generous.

Craig Ball (11)
Angmering School

WHEN I WAS YOUNG

When I was young, my mum thought I wasn't going to survive,
I had a disease called meningitis, sometimes it makes me feel
really uptightis.
I find it hard at school, but I am still cool.
I play lots of sports, at home and at school,
But I can't play rugby or contact at all.
I have an operation every four years,
Sometimes the stitches make me cry lots of tears.
I might not do well in my GCSEs
But I am getting better over the years.

Justin Charman (12)
Angmering School

ARIES

Am I Aries?
A confident Aries,
Always being heroic,
Or am I a chicken
Who won't hurt a fly?
Can I be speedy,
Always on time,
Or a lazy person, always late?
Will I risk all just for fun,
Or sit on a sofa, bored all day?
So am I an Aries?
Yes!

Joshua O'Connor-Wright (11)
Angmering School

AM I A LEO?

Am I a typical Leo?
This poem will show.
Am I faithful and loving?
I do not know.

I get encouraged into who knows what,
Driving my dad's car or sailing a yacht?
I'm sometimes loving and sometimes care
And whatever I get, I have to share.
So am I a Leo?
I still don't know.

Harry Westcott (12)
Angmering School

ZODIAC

Aquarius, Aquarius, that's what I am,
My mum is a Leo and so is my dad.
My brother is a Pisces, three of these are true.
I think my star sign is not quite me,
I'm more like a Sagittarius,
Always looking for fun and I'm also rather ambitious.
Being ambitious I always try my best,
Especially at what I want to do.
I love having fun
And I'm always laughing and giggling
And like an Aquarian,
I'm loyal to all my friends.

Kayley Alcorn (11)
Angmering School

ZODIAC

Should I be a Leo? I don't know.
This thought came upon me last night.
Frightening, striking, should I be a Virgo,
Or Libra, charming and polished?
They can talk themselves out of any woe.
Then it came to me, a Leo it was to be.
I'll find out in years to come.
Years have passed.
Faithful and loving I must be?
Now I'm older, things have changed,
Faith is the path to live,
Love is what makes the world go round.

Liam Ball (11)
Angmering School

HUMPTY DUMPTY

No problem with the ollies,
But trouble with the nollies,
The switches are complete,
But are my feet neat?
Yes for James Button.

The monkey jump is easy,
180s not so easy,
360s, now they are hard,
easier falling on some lard.
No, for James Button.

I am goofy-footed,
And it doesn't make me neat,
Buy I can do shove-its,
And you've really gotta shove-it.
Yes for James Button.

My board's United Skates,
It cost £49.99,
With ollies marks all around it,
And nollies for James Button.

My board-slides are my strong point,
50-50s much harder,
Impossible kickflip-shove-its
For James Button, champion of the world,
Until Humpty Dumpty starts skateboarding.

Sam Dickens (11)
Chichester High School For Boys

THE BAKER'S SHOP

I'll have a few currant buns,
To fill my big, lovely tum,
I'll have them with icing on,
To stuff them in. My name's John.

In the middle, it's filled with jam,
I hope it is, and not ham.
On the outside, surround with sugar
It looks so nice I can't wait.

They're so nice, I'll have some more,
Those ones there to irritate my jaw.
The baker's quite a beefy man,
No wonder he's got an empty van.

Everything on the shelves now quite tempting,
Now the shop becoming quite empty.
I'll have this one as well,
Which sent the baker in a whirl.

Nearly all my money gone,
My tummy starting to weigh a ton.
Now it's time to close the shop,
I'm now too full, I can't even hop.

The shop's locked up, the baker's gone,
The shelves are empty and I couldn't eat another one,
Till tomorrow . . .

Ben Wiggins (12)
Chichester High School For Boys

ARIES

I am the ram of the dark, night sky,
Across the sky I swiftly fly,
Confident and quick, risk all for fun,
I am the ram, I am the one.

Restless and adventurous, element of fire,
Always seeking for love and desire,
Not better or worse than anyone,
But I am the ram, I am the one.

I may be weak, but I will prevail,
Fast as a cheetah, smart as a whale,
Brain so big, can work out any sum,
'Cause I am the ram, I am the one.

David Ponsford (11)
Chichester High School For Boys

CANCER THE CRAB

He sits all day on his rock,
Doesn't move a muscle,
He just stares at the roaring waves
And gazes at the seagulls.
He wonders what it would
Be like to fly.
He has nothing to do and
Nothing to say,
That's why he sits on his rock all day.

Harry Rose (11)
Chichester High School For Boys

ZODIAC POEM

The Capricorn is very practical, whilst
Sagittarius seeks eternal joy.
Scorpio is very nippy and
Libra is charming, like James Bond.
Virgo is quite shy, but
Leo is really loving.
Cancer is really protective, whereas
Gemini is witty and youthful.
Taurus offers good protection, and
Aries is quick and confident.
Pisces is kind and sensitive, but
Aquarius is honest and loyal.
Some can be quite alike, but
Others are very different.

Ross Morton (11)
Chichester High School For Boys

LEO THE LION

Z   is for zodiac,
O   is for how obedient he is,
D   is for dream, he will lead you to yours,
I   is for how intelligent he is,
A   is for how little attitude he has,
C   is how courageous he is.

L   is for the lion in him,
E   is for how he encourages you,
O   is for how observant he is.

Joe Sanders (11)
Chichester High School For Boys

CANCER

C aring for other people when they are hurt,
A ctive like a fox after its meal, very jumpy and sprinting
   as fast as it can go.
N ice around others and obeying what he/she has been told to do,
C ool like Ali G, with Posh Spice and David Beckham on his show.
E xcellent, like Sir Isaac Newton when he discovered gravity.
R espectful to other people and their belongings.

C unning like a lion approaching its prey,
A mbitious as Michael Own was to become a professional footballer,
N asty like a tiger ripping a zebra open with its huge, sharp teeth,
C harming, like the way most ladies think Tom Cruise,
E ager as England are to win the World Cup,
R esponsible, like a waiter is for bringing your food to your table.

Tom Davis (11)
Chichester High School For Boys

ZODIAC

Z odiac is a selection of star signs that try to predict daily events,
O ften people check the text to see what their day is probably going
                              to be,
D aily the Teletext, Internet and newspapers are updated for people,
I have the star sign of Gemini, which is between the dates of
                        May 21st and June 21st.
A quarius, honest and loyal, Aquarian views life through original eyes.
C ancer, shrewd and protective, will leave nothing to chance to
                           win your love.

Paul Laparle (11)
Chichester High School For Boys

BIRTHDAY POEM

Setting off on Saturday,
We drove off north for a weekend away,
To celebrate a surprise party,
Driving cars and go-karting.
Classic cars such as E-Type and DB5
And *wow* how exciting they were to drive!

Sixty was Chris,
This we didn't want to miss.
His face was a picture as we told him the news,
Oh how did it all amuse.
A great day looking back on the past,
But like the cars, it went too fast.

Oliver Wyatt (11)
Chichester High School For Boys

ARIES

A   ries is active and moves like the wind,
R   apid like a cheetah,
I   mpressive as a lion,
E   ager and enthusiastic,
S   elf reliant as anything.

A   musing and fun to be with,
R   espectful to any human being,
I   ntelligent like a wise old owl,
E   nergetic as a cross-country runner,
S   atisfied with anything.

Jimmy Marks (11)
Chichester High School For Boys

THE STORM

The storm, the storm,
Gusting, pushing its way
To be lord of the land.

The storm, the storm,
Fighting, raining heavily,
Hitting the floor like bombs.

The storm, the storm,
Chopping trees, pounding the earth's surface
Until its heart's content, with a big bang.

The storm, the storm,
Breaking branches, flying leaves,
Droplets trembling down the windows.

The storm, the storm,
Suddenly stops as I sit and
Wipe the condensation away from the window.

Marc Baigent (11)
Chichester High School For Boys

A PLAYFUL JOURNEY

Can you walk on tiptoe as softly as a cat
And can you stamp along the road, stamp, stamp, just like that?
Can you take some great big strides just like a giant can,
Or walk along so slowly, like a poor old man?

Craig Starling (11)
Chichester High School For Boys

PET POEM

From puppies to ponies, gerbils to giraffes,
Just pick a pet, they will make you laugh.

I once had a puppy that was very, very small,
Now it's not a puppy and it's very, very tall.

Cows are big creatures, they munch on the grass,
They give us their milk and have baby calves.

Fishes are small, they swim in the sea,
I quite often have them with chips for my tea.

Cats are all fluffy, they can purr like mad,
Most of them are cute, but some can be bad.

Matt Neal (11)
Chichester High School For Boys

BURGERS

I'd like a
Big, fat,
Easy-peasy,
Lemon-squeezy,
Short and slappy,
Nice and happy,
Up and down,
Round the corner,
Double cheeseburger.
With fries on the side.

Luke Crooks (12)
Chichester High School For Boys

AWOKEN FROM THE DEAD

On a dark, gloomy night,
When it was a full moon
And I was sitting alone in my room

I heard a scary wailing sound,
It was coming from the back yard.
To make out what it was, was proving very hard.

I hope it is not him,
The zombie of the night,
Last time he came, he gave my mum a fright.

I have not seen him yet,
And I don't intend to, not tonight!
If you hear the scary, wailing sound,
I'd look out if I was you.

Martin Tizzard (11)
Chichester High School For Boys

GREEN

Some people hate the colour green,
But only beauty's what I've seen
Of nature's colour number one,
And all the good that it has done.
Its very colour gives us life,
Without it we would be in strife,
With nothing green and fresh to munch,
We'd be a very sorry bunch!
If all the hills were blue,
What would all the animals do?

Charlie Hamilton (11)
Chichester High School For Boys

SCHOOL

We go to school in the morning,
But I have to give you a warning,
We stay there till three o'clock,
After that, we get to rock.
I had a detention one day,
Then it extended to two days,
After that I started to play
And again it extended to ten days.

I started a food fight in the hall,
Everyone then thought I was cool,
The teacher stopped it rather soon,
And I was forced to the head teacher's room.

School has ended and I am glad,
Now it's time to go completely *mad!*

Daniel Yates (11)
Chichester High School For Boys

CHRISTMAS

C   andles dancing in the darkness,
H   olly berries, red, ripe and plump.
R   obin Redbreasts flying freely,
I   cicles gleaming in the winter sunlight,
S   anta's beard as white as snow and cheeks as red as Rudolf's nose,
T   urkey cooking in the oven,
M   erry Christmas, Santa shouts as he flies through the clear night sky,
A   ngels looking down from the tops of Christmas trees,
S   tockings hanging by the open fire.

Lee West (11)
Chichester High School For Boys

CARIBBEAN

We journeyed through the Caribbean Sea,
My mum, my dad, my brother and me.

The beautiful fishes, sparkling bright,
Leaping clear in the dazzling sunlight.

The island is ahead, we're nearly there,
Can't wait to get to the beaches so fair.

We swam in the water, bathed on the beach,
Dived into the water as far as I could reach.

Split open coconuts from which we drank,
Dying to see the wreck which had sunk.

James Phillips (12)
Chichester High School For Boys

NEWCASTLE POEM

Newcastle cool, Newcastle great,
Sunderland is the team I hate.
Last time we played, it was a one-one draw,
This time we've got Shearer, he's gonna score.

New boys Robert and Bellamy as well,
Dyers' coming back, we're gonna be swell.
Now if we go out and win every game
The other teams will go insane.

We're gonna win the Premiership, the FA Cup too,
We're gonna thrash everyone, including Man U!

Richard Cobb (11)
Chichester High School For Boys

RED

Red poppies trembling on the battlefield,
Red brake lights struggling to stay alive,
Red ketchup swallowing chips on the edge of the plate,
Red blood creeping beyond the plaster,
Red football shirt speeding swiftly along the field.

Red-faced, a baby screaming for its mother,
Red, the fluster of your first kiss,
Red, the twisted knot of anger,
Red, a Valentine's heart,
Red, the colour of love.

Jack Allen (11)
Chichester High School For Boys

SHADOW

Stairs creak, do I live, or do I die?
Crouch down, I see a shadow,
Am I dreaming?
I breathe heavily as I think of death,
I get a chill down my spine.
Shadow gets nearer and nearer,
I scream but I feel as though it's holding my throat.
The door slams,
My heart is racing like never before.
I switch on the light, shaking with horror,
Everything is silent.
No shadow, no noise.

Chloe Taylor (13)
Ifield Community College

IT'S COMING

It's coming, it's coming,
The thing, the thing is coming.
It's creeping up the stairs.

It's coming, it's coming,
The thing is going to get me.
I can hear it breathing.

It's coming, it's coming,
It turns the handle and enters.
It's coming, slithering along the floor.

It's breathing down my neck,
I hide further and further in my covers.

It pulls my covers.
The thing, the thing -
Is my mum.

Simone Johnston (13)
Ifield Community College

LEOPARD

L   ight glows in its eyes,
E   nergy grows through its legs,
O   btaining its prey,
P   owerful teeth when it bites,
A   round, sounds going to its ears,
R   age to the prey,
D   own the prey goes.

Jay Unwin (12)
Ifield Community College

THE SNAKE

I
Hide
In
The
Grass
And
I
Shed
My
Skin
I have all different kinds of

s

k

i

n

    Ekans a m'I ekans a m'I
    I
    a
    m
    a *snake!*

Lorna Brindley (12)
Ifield Community College

THE BEACH

One night I woke
On a dark, cold beach,
The wind howling down the sand.

I started to crawl
To the ice-cold sea,
To try to wake from this horrid dream.

Then I saw a flashing light,
I tried to reach for the light,
Then I woke and it was clear
That my dream had ended in freezing fear.

Liam Rush (13)
Ifield Community College

THE AMAZING FUTURE?

The twenty-first century,
The amazing future?
No longer daydreams,
This is reality!

Terrorist attacks,
Hijackings, bombings,
Many lives ruined.
This is happening.

Many lives taken,
Families torn apart,
Fly the flag for America,
Everyone needs support!

Armed forces preparing,
Ready to strike,
Teenagers fighting for their country,
This is life!

The twenty-first century,
The amazing future?
No longer daydreams,
This is reality!

Keith Brophy (13)
Ifield Community College

UNDER MY BED

There are creepy noises
Under my bed,
I wake up shivering.

Once I heard a loud scratching,
It came from under my bed,
I ran into Mum's room.

She took me back and
Looked under my bed,
Everywhere but under the box.

There it was again,
Scratch! Scratch!
I ran back into Mum's room.

I was screaming,
'It is still there,
It's still there!'

I made Mum search
Under my bed again.
'There's nothing there so go to sleep.'

Scratch! Scratch!
It was still there,
I plucked up some courage

Took a deep breath and . . .

There it was, under the box,
The one Mum didn't check.
It was still scratching.

It saw me and
Jumped on my shoulder
And started licking me.

'Oh Socks, stop licking me.'
It was only Socks,
My cat.

Simone Arnold (13)
Ifield Community College

IF I WERE . . .

If I were a fly,
Which I'm not nor am I,
I would fly anywhere,
But I couldn't eat a pear.

If I were a bird,
Which I'm not, I have heard,
I would dance for all four seasons
And I could sing for no reason.

If I were a bunny,
Which I'm not, it sounds funny,
I would dance and play
And bounce all day.

If I were all three,
Which I'm not, I am me,
I would have lots of time
And that would be fine.

Hayley Craven (12)
Ifield Community College

SHADOWS

As I lay here in my bed
In the dark night,
The wind is howling,
Trees are rustling.

I hear a noise,
A loud noise,
Like waves crashing.
Through the moonlight a shadow forms.

It's wiggly and slithers
From where it hides.
Long bands of darkness surround
Egg-like shape.

I can feel it on my skin
As it touches and rocks me.
From nowhere, another band of darkness
Joins us, rocking me harder.

I hear a voice in the distance,
Calling my name.
As it stir, the voice gets stronger, louder,
I begin to recognise the voice, it's my mother.

Danielle Farley (14)
Ifield Community College

THE SEA

The sea is many different colours glistening in the sun,
It holds a lot of secrets down in its depths.
Strange creatures roaming around,
Fishes swimming up and down,
Calm waves lapping the shore.

The crystal clear sea glistens in the sun,
Big boats, little boats, bobbing on the sea,
While underneath, the current emerges,
Large waves appear,
Then all is still and quiet.

Kelly Williams (12)
Ifield Community College

A DREAM OF HALLOWE'EN

At night,
I have put the light
On my torch,
My torch was very bright.

In my bedroom,
It was a dark room,
Because it was night-time.

When I was asleep,
I had a dream.
I gave a scream.

My mother came upstairs.
When my mother had gone,
I had a dream again.

My dream
Was full of ghosts,
Full of witches,
Full of mummies,
Full of skeletons
And full of pumpkins.
It was Hallowe'en!

Karen Wan (13)
Ifield Community College

H₂O

H$_2$O has got to go,
Even though it makes plants grow!
It floods the rivers,
The streams run fast,
The damage done,
It can be vast!

It falls from the clouds
And showers the world,
It fills the oceans,
It glistens like pearls.
It runs down the mountains,
To the lakes full of swirls.

The world needs water,
The plants and the trees,
All of the animals,
The birds and bees.

H$_2$O has got to go?
I don't think so - it helps plants grow!

Stephanie Clark (13)
Ifield Community College

A BIG FRIGHT

Once on a dark, dark night,
Something gave me quite a fright,
What it was, I don't know,
But it put up quite a show.

Bright lights flashed
And then I dashed.
What it was, I don't care,
All I know is now it's not there.

Now I'm home and it is gone,
But I'm still shaking to the bone.
Mum and Dad said with a smirk,
'You were frightened by a firework.'

Sarah Harris (13)
Ifield Community College

PASSIONATE HEARTBREAK

Glorious rays of crystal-white light
Reflect into his sparkling green eyes.
His lonely lips desiring a comforting kiss,
His deserted heart reaching for a friend.

Tightly I hold his body against mine,
Never wanting to let go of this passionate moment.
My garden lit,
Like a firefly in the clear black sky.

All fears disappear as I am in his presence.
The wind flows gently through the midnight sky,
Avoiding the glistening stars.

Without warning, vision of the moon has gone,
Replaced by thick clouds of painful thunder.
Skies flash like an electric eel,
As I turn and realise he's vanished.

Nowhere to run, life seems pointless.
I'll beat the agonising pain,
The endless tears,
As I know he is gone forever.
He is never coming back.

Carly Welch (14)
Ifield Community College

THE HIPPY DREAM

'Peace' and 'love' you could hear them cry,
With their beads, long hair and shirts with tie-dye.
However ridiculous it now may seem,
This was all part of the Hippy Dream.

Bob Dylan, The Beatles, artists like those,
They too wore the hippy-trippy clothes.
Handing out flowers on London's Kings Road,
Going to 'love-ins' and 'peace-ins' by the load.

The press said they were dirty and bad,
Their mums and dads said they were mad.
Visiting a pop festival in San Francisco,
That was one cool place they had to go.

Now everyone laughs at the hippys' work,
Dismissing them as eccentric drop-outs in flowery shirts,
But they all missed the most important thing;
Peace - why didn't they listen?

Alice Crane (13)
Ifield Community College

I POLISH

I polish the tables every Monday
I polish Grandpa's ears
I polish the months and the days
I polish the smells and the fears.

I polish Grandpa's specs
I polish the lies and the truth
I polish your funniest secrets
I polish my old mate, Ruth.

I polish the land of angels
The tail of the horse too
If you think this poem is rubbish
Then I'll come round an d polish off you.

Vicky Nash (12)
Ifield Community College

FIRST DAY AT SCHOOL

Got to dash, I mustn't be late,
The bell has gone, it's half-past eight.
Straighten my tie, tuck in my shirt,
Got to look smart and be alert.

Masses of faces rushing about,
Some very quiet and some always shout.
Make for the classroom, I see my tutor,
I hope today I will use the computer.

I look at my planner, what do I see?
We have maths, English and PSVE.
Maths is first with Mr White,
I hope I did my homework right.

The lesson has finished, thank goodness for that,
I meet my friends and have a good chat,
Back from break, onto PE,
I don't want to fall and graze my knee.

Last lesson approaches, I hope it goes quickly,
I'm getting a headache and feeling quite sickly!
Out of school, on my way home,
Ring, ring, ring, goes my mobile phone.

Gemma Heath (12)
Ifield Community College

MURDER

Did I experience remorse, grief or regret
As you fell?
Of course I did,
I know those emotions well.

There is no training
For what I have done,
All my self-pity
Is long gone.

I want the works,
Sent down for years,
Not some judge
Who sees my tears.

For though I am sad,
With your last breath,
I have revenge
Through your death.

Ross Brophy (13)
Ifield Community College

THE GHOSTLY GRAVEYARD

I was walking in the graveyard
Late one dark and dingy night,
When I heard a spooky, eerie noise
Which gave me such a fright!

I trembled and I shook with fear,
I saw a vampire in front of me,
With big fangs and a sword,
I hoped I wouldn't be his tea.

I ran as fast as I could,
Hoping he would go away,
But he chased me until I fell in a hole,
I knew I'd never see the light of day!

Leanne Fitzgibbon (13)
Ifield Community College

HEARTBROKEN

The day you said we couldn't be together,
I felt my life would end,
Without you by my side,
I cried and cried for days on end.

Whenever I see you, I want you back in my arms,
Where you belong,
Memories come flooding back to me,
The good times we had together.

It tears me up inside
That we can never be together again
How I wish that we could be together,
The way things used to be.

But you are with someone new,
It turns me inside out,
I try and try, oh how I try to get you out of my mind,
But you keep creeping back in,
Thinking about you day and night.

Now you have moved on,
I suppose I should move on too,
But there will always be a special place for you in my heart,
Love for you always.

Carley Wenham (13)
Ifield Community College

THIS CAN NEVER BE

Our red kiss of passion
Was like water against paper,
The stones in our hearts cast
To the bottom of the bleak sea.
We knew that our partners'
Hearts would be crushed,
Like crimson petals, as the petals
Fall to the ground, their hearts
Become anchors.
Our strange passion
Was under the shining of the moon.
Reflecting in his eyes the moon glistened
Our colours of love, created a rainbow
Of colours, which only we could see.
The longing pain to tell our partners
Grew inside me, but we knew our
Love and passion was doomed,
A web had been spun between us,
Our lives faded from us,
Our secret fell to the bottom of the sea.

Claire Wilkinson (14)
Ifield Community College

FRIENDS

My mates are really great,
They are there for me when I'm in a state,
We have a lot of fun when we go out,
We always have a scream and shout.

There are so many reasons why my friends are always there,
No other bullies give me a scare,
I hope we all stay friends forever,
Because we are all great friends when we're together.

When I am down and feeling blue,
They tell me just what to do!
We go out all the time,
Which makes me want to rhyme.

Jennifer Farrell (13)
Ifield Community College

MOTHER

She who wakes early
To start the day
Wanders the silent house
Barely enough noise
To awaken the household
Just enough to wake the dog.

Solemnly walks down the stairs
Gets her breakfast
And walks the dog.
Back she comes to finish her jobs.

Off to work she goes
To face her daily tasks
Merrily in the morning.
She phones home to
Awaken the family
And to hear their happy voices.

Back to the daily task
After listening to their happy voices.
Happily she works, watching the clock,
Waiting for 2 o'clock.
Time for home,
The family time begins.

Lena Robinson (13)
Ifield Community College

THE MOTH

First, I am falling out of love,
Falling giddy out of the gown I put on,
To take it off, out of lace
And satin underthings, hooked and eyed.

As if they were the object.
I am falling out of the lamplight,
Whose those nothings lie,
Beautifully.

Empty puddles after rain,
Falling out of that wave tickling,
Constant time against my heart.

Out of mind.
There is my last room
Which I am falling out of:
Only a lamp,

A clean desk, floor scrubbed bare,
One door to latch and lock,
Bed sheets pulled up tight enough to hold me,
Falling into sleep like a stone.

Amy Young (14)
Ifield Community College

FACES

My room was dark and spooky,
I was laying in my bed,
Peeking from behind my covers,
Scary faces running through my head.

Curtains blowing through the open window,
Slam the door closes with a bang,
The bright moon turned to a dull and creepy face
And then a sound . . . *clang!*

My creaky door opens,
I hide under my covers,
I take a little peek
And there were two lovers.

Kellie Nichols (13)
Ifield Community College

LIFE'S JOURNEY

Crying witness, painful tear,
Melting sun, slice of ice.

Distant memory, engraved,
Mirage, empty expectations.

Cold gaze, unforgiving,
Dismal.

Declining desire,
Daggers in smiles.

Heartless, cruel life,
Speeding time.

Powerful dream, revealing credulity,
Regretting life.

Hoping forgiveness, changing fate.

Altering goals, desires,
Priorities in life.

Life's test, beyond limits,
Successful end.

Glimmer of light, floating hope,
Eternal paradise.

Amina Haq (17)
Ifield Community College

SUNSET BEACH

The blue, wavy ocean
Moves rapidly from side to side,
Dolphins flip through the air,
Splashing into the white waves.

The waves splash over the golden sand,
Making it sparkle like a star,
In the glistening shadow of the sunlight
Through my crystal blue eyes.

My crystal eyes can see
The reflection of the sun,
Beaming down on the shells,
Revealing a sunset.

The sunset slowly disappears
Behind the ocean,
The beautiful colours blend together,
Making purple and pinks.

Danielle Andrews (14)
Ifield Community College

THE DISASTER PARTY

The ghost goes moaning down the hall,
Down the stairs and to the ball.
He meets his friends and begins to dance,
But really it is more of a prance!

The orchestra strikes up a tune,
Through the window shines the moon.
Into the kitchen floats the ghost,
Oh no, he's burnt the toast!

One disaster after another,
Then he spots his dear old mother.
Shock, horror, oh no, out jump Mum's false teeth,
Yet another disaster, they land in the beef!

Oh no, what's that hideous smell?
It seems to be Uncle Tel.
He slipped in the sewer in a panic,
Now he's driving everyone manic!

Gemma Coston (13)
Ifield Community College

MY BEST FRIEND

My best friend is Fyona,
She's always there for me,
She helps me with my problems,
She's always there and always will be.

We have known each other for years,
We've had good times and bad,
I've helped her too,
She says I'm the best friend she's ever had.

Fyona has had rough times,
I've helped her through her tears,
Because she is my best friend
And has been there through the years.

She's always been there for me,
Fyona is a really good friend,
She'll always be there for me,
Right up to the end.

Holly Marshall (13)
Ifield Community College

Out Of School

It's 3:00,
No more XX crosses,
No more teachers
Being the bosses.

Stacks of homework,
Get it done
Before it gets dark,
So I can have some fun.

Whip that tie off,
Shirt's come out,
Before the teachers
Have a shout.

No more computer games,
Homework first,
Gotta tell your friends,
Homework comes first!

Beverly Wells (13)
Ifield Community College

War

War is a terrible, terrible thing,
Just think of all the pain and suffering it can bring,
I would give my life to end this war,
Because it would end all the chaos and hatred and more.

It would be great if this war could end,
Then all the countries could all be friends,
But instead I'm stuck in this dark, dank cell,
With rotting corpses and a putrid smell.

It feels like this war will go on forever more,
With all these people dying in vain,
And I dream the day when I will be free,
And when the whole world will see how stupid they have been.

Callum Watts (12)
Ifield Community College

THE LONELY GHOST

Down the stairs and out of the door,
Through the forest and onto the moor,
Where a lonely ghost will wait,
Standing there till very late.

Wishing, hoping for a friend,
That an angel will hopefully send,
Alive or dead he doesn't care,
Old friend, new friend with stories to share.

Day and night, there he stays,
Dark and light for many days,
Never changing, always the same,
Never moving through wind and rain.

If he stays for long enough,
Though it will be very tough,
Maybe the angel will answer his prayers
And send someone who really cares.

Down the stairs and out of the door,
Through the forest and onto the moor,
There you'll see a lonely ghost
Hoping for something he wants most,
A friend.

Sarah Grubb (13)
Ifield Community College

THE ATROCIOUS 21ST CENTURY

Into the 21st century and people said no more wars
And that everybody will obey the new laws.
The atrocities have begun and it's all got out of hand,
The problems are complicated, but some are just about land.

Suddenly people are mourning for their loved ones.
Terrorist attacks flood the world with hijackings and bombs
Crash! Bang! Buildings pulverised to their foundations,
The American symbols are lost; lost forever.

Young teenagers run riot, wreaking havoc,
However, it's not their fault, they are just fighting for their side.
These kids only get an education of how to fight and kill,
All this for what? Who controls the land.

Into the 21st century and people said no more wars
And that everybody will obey the new laws.
The atrocities have begun and it's all got out of hand,
The problems are complicated, but some are just about land.

Rachit Singhal (14)
Ifield Community College

BEFORE SCHOOL

I opened my eyes, full of sleep,
Bath water running, hot and deep.
Downstairs in the kitchen my breakfast is cooking,
Upstairs in the bedroom for homework I'm looking.

We go in all weather, in sunshine or storms,
Wandering to school in our new uniforms.
Arriving in school we sit on the bench,
What's our first less? Miss Mayo for French.

While we're sitting here waiting, the bell starts to sound,
So we head for our tutor, heels dragging the ground.
He calls registration and we all shout, 'Here,'
The start of the school day is about to appear.

I pick up my bag and head on my way,
The teachers are ready for the start of the day.
I walk in my class as I hear Teacher say,
'This is your task for today.'

Faye Rabson (12)
Ifield Community College

SCHOOL

First day at school,
Nerves as big as basketballs,
Walking with friends,
Going round corners and bends.

I walked in the class,
Teacher's hair covered in grass,
I thought it was funny,
So she took my dinner money.

Me and my mate had maths first,
I thought it couldn't get worse,
This was because I had a double cross,
Then she strictly demanded, she was the boss.

The clock struck three
I desperately wanted to pee.
I end this poem, short but sweet,
I will go home to eat that delightful meat.

Chris Charvill (12)
Ifield Community College

ANOTHER GLOOMY DAY

The sun, glinting on the dewy roof tops,
The clouds, dancing on a calm, calm sea,
The buildings looming with the rustling treetops,
And me knowing where I want to be.

The classroom full of bored pupils,
A headache jumping from head to head,
A child told to take 'these two pills,'
To 'go home' and 'lay in your bed.'

The colours from beyond the window,
The sound coming from the gaps,
The life coming from the outside, though
Children singing 'new-age raps.'

The laughing from the giggly schoolgirl,
The football from the sixth form boys,
The boys that with their insults hurl,
And children playing with their toys.

A normal day at a normal school,
But a new day will be dawning,
With people walking to their school
At half-eight in the morning.

Holly Webb (13)
Ifield Community College

THE STORY OF HOW I STOPPED WATCHING TV

My telly and my couch are my two best friends,
I sit and watch them weekdays, the same for weekends.
So many choices and so many voices, I don't know what to watch,
There are a few soaps, a documentary and a bit of news,
And if I'm feeling hungry, I'll flick to a recipe.

But now I have found something new, I think it's called a book
I took a glance, then I looked and at that moment I was hooked.
It's just like a TV, but it taught me how to cook,
I take it with me wherever I go,
But if someone asks me, 'What's on TV?'
I'll just reply, 'I don't know!'

Lauren Martin (12)
Ifield Community College

THE VOYAGE TO LIBERTY

I am trapped in your web of greed,
I am china in bubble wrap.
I wish to be placed upon life's
Broad shelf of liberty.
Like shattered glass broken from the window
That shields your insecurities,
I wish to be free.
From the forest's unclenched hand comes
The beast of reality raising its ugly head.
Like a fly trapped in your web,
I am thrust upon a rose bed.
In the process of smelling them,
I am entangled and pierced by thorns,
Filling up with poison
From your destructive heart.
Barriers block my way and
The wizard's wand breaks them.
I am perched on the rim of a cauldron.
Will I topple into the unknown?
No, I step out into the fairy tale
And my journey to the happy ending begins.

Sophie Dowdeswell (14)
Ifield Community College

I'LL ALWAYS CARE

Forever will my heart be true,
Rejoicing in my love for you.
Acknowledging your love for me,
Sensing we will always be.
Every day you make me glad,
Reflecting on the fun we've had.

Rapt in joy and desire for you,
Accordingly we'll see it through.
Yielding not to pressures we've found,
My heart and yours are fastly bound.
Only we know the love we share,
Never can there be a better pair,
Dedicated to you, I'll always care.

Tracey Brown (17)
Ifield Community College

APOCALYPSE

All I could see in the distance was a sea of them
Far, far away,
Then they were everywhere,
Waves and waves of them,
Swarming around me,
They smashed
And smashed
Into the ground,
Killing themselves,
Killing everything,
It was . . .
Apocalypse.

Paul Bellchambers (14)
Ifield Community College

31ˢᵗ OCTOBER

A spooky night, time to come and play,
31ˢᵗ October is one of the creepiest days.
Children dress up as monster and much more,
Everyone dresses up, even the people who are poor.
Doorbells ring,
Children sing,
'Trick or treat?'
Chocolate, lollies or any candy,
Everyone thinks people who have got candy are pretty handy.

Pumpkins are orange and now have a face,
Everywhere you go, they're all over the place.
Witches, bats, cats and rats,
All scare me to death, especially witches' pointy hats.
You must be in denial
If you think they are not vile.
The full moon is fading,
And no more time for sweet-trading.
The clock strikes twelve, it's all over,
Back to bed, tucked up with my teddy called Clover.
Sleep, sleep and sleep,
Back to reality.

Sarah Grant (13)
Ifield Community College

BLUE

The blue reminds me of the sea,
Also reminds me of the sky,
The flowers remind me of the sweetness
Of my mum.

Ricky White (12)
Ifield Community College

THE SANDMAN

Someone's climbing up the stairs,
The little boy for whom no one cares,
The moon shines down on a shaking bed,
The floors are creaking, no one's dead,
The lamp burns out, someone comes,
The creaking door opens slowly,
It's his mum.
She tucks him in bed
And pats him on the head
And he slowly falls asleep.
Then a tall shadow creeps,
The sandman does a funny jig,
Across the room like a thin jumping twig,
Wakes the boy up with a weird smile,
The little boy scared,
The sandman throws a sand pile.
The boy's eyes are weak, he wants to scream,
The sandman flies away with all the boy's dreams.

Dee-Dee Edlin (14)
Ifield Community College

NIGHTMARE POEM

The night was dark as the black hole,
The stars were like dead people looking at me,
Suddenly out of the eclipse.
Thunder made a big bang like a gunshot,
I shake like I have been put in the freezer,
It was like my heart, soul and my skeleton
Came out of my skin.

Amir Aslam (13)
Ifield Community College

In The Attic

In the attic,
In a corner, there lies
Something under a blanket
That only comes out at night.
I hear it calling my name
Through the floorboards,
But no one believes me.
One night, I went up there,
I saw shadows moving,
The light went out,
A cold shiver came over me.
There it was,
Standing right in front of me.

This poem was not finished
Because Sophie was found with no head.
She had been murdered,
The case remains open.

Hayley Fowlie & Simone Arnold (13)
Ifield Community College

A Heart's Soul

Love goes on its travels too far, it never stops until it drops.
Love is true, love is alive, love is a heart that never says goodbye.
No love is real, but love is everything. It never dies down.
It stays the same throughout your whole life.
Love can be anything, it makes you feel a special something.
How is love here? How is love there? But what is love?
I don't know, just something.

Rebecca Stoner (12)
Ifield Community College

BLOOD

Blood, blood, blood all around,
Eyes popping out,
Blood spitting out,
Eyes all over the place,
Fingers falling off,
Dancing around the room,
Jumping off and on,
Blood all around, blood all around,
Spitting everywhere.

Puddles, puddles, puddles of blood,
Fingers, nails, eyes and teeth,
Blood pouring out of mouths
Like a waterfall,
Hearts, liver pouring out,
Through the waterfall.

Suzanne Brown (13)
Ifield Community College

THE NIGHTMARE

The night was dark as a black hole,
The stars were brightly shining in the night,
The lamp came on when the sun went down,
When the children were sleeping and the sandman was flying.
The whole night was blinding,
There were bright red eyes coming from the sky,
There were the sounds of claws scraping along,
The bats were screeching and the vampires were biting.
When the sun came up and the children woke,
All was right again.

Jolie Clark (13)
Ifield Community College

THE TWIN TOWERS

The Twin Towers stood tall,
Watching over the land,
People came from far and wide
To see a sight so grand.

People stood and gazed at the wonder,
'Look how high they go.'
'How long do your reckon they'll stand?'
The people would say, 'Who knows?'

As the towers stood posing for the public,
They didn't see the tragedy coming.
One more picture taken,
Then everyone started running.

The plane had crashed into the building,
The building that once was so tall.
Everyone watched as the mighty building
Began to fall.

Another plane had crashed
Into another mighty tower
People watched in horror
As it fell like a helpless flower.

The main attraction
Was now a heap of rubble,
The air was full of dust,
Someone's in deep trouble.

Nobody was found in the heap,
Hundreds of people are gone,
Everyone is in shock
That two Twin Towers are done!

Sarah Tonna (14)
Ifield Community College

MY OLD SCHOOL

I remember my old school,
The teachers were all so kind,
My classroom was really small,
The toilets were hard to find.

First there was Mrs Whinder,
She was OK to me,
But she was sometimes bossy,
She wouldn't let us free.

Then there was in year five,
I had about a load,
Mrs Bain, Mr Beeston and Mrs I,
Mr Beeston looked like a toad.

Then in year six, Mrs Sudan,
She was the most fun,
She was rather understanding,
She liked my dad and mum.

Then in year 7, Mr T,
He was nice, smart, weird and funny,
He was never, ever sad,
Even when I was really bad.

Mr H was as bright as a berry,
He never was sad,
He was really funny,
He was the best I had.

I miss my old school sometimes,
But I have the best class ever,
I'll always remember my school
With the bestest teachers ever.

Amie Edge (12)
Ifield Community College

THE MOUNTAINOUS MOON

It's round, bright and grey,
You can see it at night and sometimes day.
I travels around us
Without making any fuss.
It's always the same distance away!

No creatures have been found
On this spacious ground.
Humans have been on it,
All prepared with their kit,
Couldn't make any sound!

The first was Neil Armstrong,
Who wasn't there for very long.
He put down his flag
And left with his bag,
He must have been quite strong!

I found it wasn't naturally bright,
Because the sun gave off all its light.
The bumpy bits looked like mountains,
Shaped like erupted fountains,
Which was quite a sight!

There isn't any gravity on this grey ball,
Don't worry, you can't really fall,
But it's best to bring your own breathing equipment,
You could run out at that last moment
And there will be no one to call!

Have you found out
What I've been talking about?
It's the moon, of course,
More precious than a horse!

Priya Patel (13)
Ifield Community College

SADISTIC (OR DO YOU MEAN MASOCHISTIC)

Sometimes I have a nightmare,
A scare that I enjoy,
The mind of a powerful spirit,
But I don't fear it.
Why does it want to scare a boy?
Nightmares predict the future,
Send a warm shiver down my spine,
See, I'm not afraid
Of thoughts and the power of the mind.
Through this comes my new inner strength,
No more midnight waking
In fear, in tears and sweat,
But I'll describe the rest.

Why is this ghost trying to change my life?
I'm not afraid to fight back,
Is it a dream or a sacrifice?
I'm not scared to die
From this thing which will change me,
Replace me,
It will not embrace me.
My feelings are not fear, no tears,
In fact, lots of smiles and cheers,
No quiver in the chest,
A joy unlike the rest.
A joy that's masochistic,
It will suffer a sadistic pain. Who's insane?
This is just normal, bizarre it may seem,
This is just a spirit one cannot see.
Who is sadistic, him or me?

Erfan Ullah (13)
Ifield Community College

LIKE A BIRD

Her metallic body starts to glide,
She takes off, veering to one side,
Taking tourists to their destination,
Rising high with no hesitation.
Like a bird she flies through the clouds,
Her engines roar making loud sounds,
The sunlight shines off of her wing,
The quiet engine starts to sing.
Looking from the window at the sea below,
Speeding up, yet nobody seems to know,
She makes many people glad,
Yet sometimes she is bad.
As she beings to get lower,
Her engines become slower,
She releases carefully each landing gear,
The passengers become tense with fear.
Bump, bump, bump, she hits the ground,
Vehicles and men gather around,
With hustle and bustle they walk off.
Dusk arrives as the sun sets,
Rest she does not, she starts her jets,
She restarts the journey,
To arrive the next day, very early!

Paul Longhurst (13)
Ifield Community College

MOVING TO HONG KONG

I don't want to go,
Why should I have to?
I'm scared!

What about my family?
What about my friends?
I'm worried!

What will school be like?
What will my house be like?
I'm excited!

What will the food be like?
Noodles and egg fried rice,
How nice!

When will I see my nephew?
And the baby that's not yet born?
I'm sad.

What will my lessons be like?
Will I have to speak Chinese?
I'm annoyed!

What will I be doing there?
What will my life be like?
What an adventure!

Gary Neale (12)
Ifield Community College

THE DISASTER

We are sorry to those we cannot get our help to,
Sometimes it just makes me think, 'What can I do?'
You're the first on my mind,
We just need to leave the bad behind.
The way I feel is so unreal,
We really need to try and chill.

The really bad disasters are leaving people in plasters.
Our families die, all of us cry.
It's tearing us apart
And breaking our hearts.
Now the bad
Should suffer as we had.
Police fight,
But no one's all right.
The bad are laughing,
Whilst our hearts are halving.

Sarah Baldwin (12)
Ifield Community College

THE END IS HERE

The end is here,
The streets lay bare,
The ghostly white moon
Lays in its black grave.
The stars gathered on Orion's Belt,
All watching and waiting.
The wicked waves
All fight for their survival,
A deafening silence echoes
The beginning of the end is here.

Neal Patel (15)
Ifield Community College

A Tale Of Two Castles

Alone, I walk through the Bloody Tower,
Crowds jostle me, yet I walk alone.
I hear not the sound of conversation,
Nor the click of a camera flash,
Instead I hear the rustle of silken gowns,
The sound of an axe blade biting wood,
Slicing human flesh and sinew,
Exacting miserable punishment.
I see not the hordes of tourists in brightly coloured clothes,
Nor the colourful displays giving names and dates and places,
Instead I see shades of bygone battles,
Glittering gems and bloodstained robes.
I smell not the aroma of well-packed picnics,
Nor the mingling of scents and perfumes,
Instead I smell the nauseating stench of rotting flesh,
The smell of blood and fear and death.

Michelle Barnett (12)
Ifield Community College

Poem

Black war proceeds in a box of lies
Who kill their prey in a dark seed.
Blood lies in the sand under a rosebush,
Windows find empty sleep
With lovers light.
Murder's high pledge
Through life's miseries.
Empty rooms shine through
Before power balls
Raise up ending life
In one swift stroke.

Mark Maskell (15)
Ifield Community College

I AM AWAKE ALL NIGHT

There's a creak on the stairs,
My arms get prickly hairs,
I jump with fright
And stay awake all night.
I hear the most,
Is there a ghost?
I look around,
Nothing I found.
I look at the end of my bed,
I see a head.
A hand comes from under,
I hear thunder.
Something is bright,
My mum's just turned on the light.

Leena Patel (13)
Ifield Community College

HORROR POEM

Moving slowly in the dark,
Street lights flickering like a lighter's spark,
Wild wind blowing in the night,
Bone-breaking bangs giving you a fright.
Creaking on the old wooden stairs,
Hiding under the bed covers as the sandman glares,
Suddenly you hear a yelp
And a poor young boy cries for help.
The sandman snatched his eyes
And flew away into the deep, dark sky!

Tracey Woolford (14)
Ifield Community College

THE PERPETUAL ISLAND

The passionate island in the jungle of sea
Has violet sand and a rose-red tree.
The sun rains onto sunbathing crabs
And the dancing corals entertain the ocean.
Melodramatic fish watch a theatrical performance,
Palm trees salsa to the singing wind.
Depressed, washed up shells start crying on the beach,
The obsessed sun goes to sleep
When the nocturnal moon wakes up.
However the stars come out to play,
The waves move on and the tide goes home.
The island sprints to sleep.

Naomi West (15)
Ifield Community College

SEPARATION

The fire fearlessly burnt
Our love from each other's smiles
Causing us to live in a painful darkness
Away from what was once a well-earned love
But now nothing but an eternal death.
As love meets hatred
And hatred meets love,
They collide with one another
And drain all hope of togetherness once again
From my heart,
Separating us: apart.

Joanne Chapman (14)
Ifield Community College

THE BAT

Pointy ears listening for prey,
Wings like bony cloaks,
Soft, grey fur,
Nose like a horseshoe,
Blind as a bat,
Communicating by screeching.

Daniel Kania (12)
Ifield Community College

WAR

W ar is a time when a country comes together or splits apart,
A ftermath, the devastation and destruction, disease and poverty
that follows a war.
R elief when the war ends.

Stephen Weston (12)
Ifield Community College

CHEETAH

Shining gold with black spots,
Strong and wild,
Sharp and quick as lightning,
Piercing eyes,
Moving slowly, but surely
Towards its prey,
Round they go,
Determined, always on the move.

Chris Kizza (12)
Ifield Community College

TAINTED LOVE

The dark circles around my love
Smashing like a china puzzle
Arrested passion
Crooked heart
Lightning crosses my mind
My pounding heart
Surrenders to the hot, burning flames.

Joanne Nash (14)
Ifield Community College

MINT STARS

The mint petal of the flower
Shines white in the moon.
Pieces fall to the ground like burning embers
And the stem cries silent tears.
With her petals shed, lipstick is cast across her lips
The other discarded petals emerge as
Tiny sky-bound stars.

Nicola Wenham (14)
Ifield Community College

TIGERS

Tigers are stripy,
Like the long grass, yellow grass.
A tiger's eyes glow in the night.
Tigers run fast
As light,
Well, as fast as a sports car.

Ros February (12)
Ifield Community College

NIGHT FRIGHT

I remember the night in November,
It was a cold and dark night without anyone in sight.
I have tried to forget it with all my might, as I recall there was no light.
Walking all wrapped up tight, I walked into the night.

As I walked down the dark alleyway, I could hear footsteps behind me.
Far away at first, but stalking with thirst.
The footsteps were gaining ground behind me as my heart began
to pound.
I experienced the fear without shedding a tear,
I found that looking at the ground would block out the sound.
My pain was increasing with every drop of rain,
As thunder roared into the night, I was a sight of fright.
Louder and louder with every step of the way,
My heart was thumping and my blood was pumping.

The footsteps behind me were coming closer,
I began to think of the impending danger.
My head was going manic as I began to panic,
I tried to forget the pain in order to keep me sane.
I began to leap and trying not to weep,
As I began to wonder, 'Why can't I be stronger?'
I could not bear this any longer.

I heard a voice shout, 'Stop!' as my temperature reached the top.
As I awoke, my sister spoke.
As I saw the light beam, I realised it was a dream,
It seemed so real as I began to appeal.
As I reached for the lamp, I could still feel the damp,
I felt so cold as I lay in the mould,
I was sleepless and I felt so restless.
As morning came near, my fear began to disappear.

Nasima Kada (13)
Ifield Community College

DEATH COMES IN MANY DISGUISES

There you would lie, all still and cold
I'd remember the stories that you once told,
Your friends and beloved would weep and cry
That's what would happen if you were to die.

But you are not dead, so sing and dance
You have been given another chance,
So seize this gift as if it were your last,
Live in the future and not in the past.

You can do all the things that you dare,
You can live your life without a care,
But be careful, because life is full of surprises
And death comes in many disguises.

So make sure that you get your fill,
The time will come to pay the bill,
Your life is a very high price to pay,
I don't know what I'd do if you went away.

I tried to warn you, but you did not see
Just how much you meant to me
And now you lie in that awful bed,
I feel suicidal because you are now dead.

There you now lie, all still and cold
I remember the stories that you once told,
Your friends and beloved now weep and cry,
That's what happened when you did die.

Rebecca Jones (13)
Ifield Community College

ALONE

Alone in the house,
The very dark house,
I heard a creaking far away,
Getting nearer and louder,
Coming closer and closer.
I was shaking,
I could feel its breathing
Moving the hairs on my neck.
Gently, coldly it touched me,
I shot up in bed,
Looked around,
No one there.
Scared and shaking,
I could still hear creaking
Coming closer, closer,
Closer into my room.
'Who are you?'
No answer.
I looked, I screamed,
It touched me again.
I snapped open my eyes,
What is happening?
The creaking came closer and closer,
It touched me.
I stopped breathing.

Joanne Pullen (13)
Ifield Community College

MY LITTLE SISTERS?
(Dedicated to Saskia (5 years old) and Megan (9 years old)
Burtenshaw)

I don't remember when you were young, I was young too
I remember when your baby sister was.
We played on the beach,
Your baby sister would call me a 'that'
Because she couldn't say my name.

Now you're nine and your sister's five,
You're all grown up,
You're very tall,
You're gorgeous,
You're beautiful.

I love you so much,
We leave good times behind, but there are many to come!
I never have bad times when you're around,
Your smiles light up my world!

I'll do anything to make you happy,
I hope I never make you sad,
I will always be glad to have you around,
You're just two people I've grown up with,
But I love you so much.

You're like my little sisters
Who I will always adore and care for.

Emma Barling (13)
Ifield Community College

THE SNAKE

I am the holder of the mysteries of life,
I am the answer,
The nectar,
The treasure.
Reach into my jaws for what you seek.
You may have raised me,
You may put me in a cage,
But I am still the evil reptile,
Immortally confined to scales.

Befriend me,
Care for me,
Lower your guard.
A second is all it takes.

My true character is exposed only when I strike.
Jab,
Sin,
Constrict,
Wickedness,
Engulf,
Malice.

I am cunning and elusive,
The shadow of the animal kingdom,
The dark memory in the white soul.

Jonathan Baldry (14)
Ifield Community College

THE WEEPING WIDOW

The fire drenched
By the watery green waves
Of the forest that suffers
In silence.

Stripped of clothes,
The weeping black bodies
Stand short and jagged.

Blankets of steam
Wilt the heavy emerald leaves,
As they recline wounded and blistered.

Shedding skin,
Veins ripped apart,
Endless black,
An empty hole.

The torn forest soul
Cries heavy tears
That fall and shatter,
As they drown the forest floor.

The tears lay like crystals,
Then spread into tiny mirrors
That reflect the above.
An evil reflection.

Charlotte Walker (15)
Ifield Community College

THE CREATURE IS . . .

The creature comes out only at night,
It only comes out when it wants a fight.
The creature comes out only at night,
It only comes out when the timing is right.

The creature is small and light,
It jumps around at a great big height.
The creature is small and light,
The creature's skin is very tight.

The creature can't be found out in the day,
It lives around in clumps of hay.
The creature can't be found out in the day,
It's quite sweet if I must say.

The creature is quiet and small,
It can get into a great big mall.
The creature is quiet and small,
But it can also live in a massive hall.

The creature has a long, thin tail,
It can glide around like a sail.
The creature has a long, thin tail,
Which helps it get home without fail.

The creature makes a squeaking sound,
Which can echo all around.
The creature makes a squeaking sound,
The creature is a mouse that can be found.

Elaine Willoughby (13)
Ifield Community College

Summer Fling

The day I left I cried and cried
For what would never be,
It was probably all in my head,
You never wanted me.

The lonely nights spent thinking,
Your face clear in my head,
But to you I am just forgotten,
You think of her instead.

My friends say I should forget it,
Stop wasting time on you,
But only I know how I felt,
And I still feel it deeply too.

One day I will be over you
And get on with my life,
But I hope I will never see you
With a girlfriend, fiancée or wife.

I know it is pathetic,
I still feel that special thing
And I hope that in the future,
I will forget my summer fling.

Charlotte Ellis (14)
Ifield Community College

MY TREAT

Going to the shop with my money,
£20 in my wallet,
Jump on my petrol scooter,
Flying past a barking dog,
A runaway cat,
My friends walking down the road,
A line of parked cars,
Round the corner into the car park,
Open the door,
Pick up a trolley,
Gobstoppers and sherbet,
Teddy Bears, liquorice laces,
Thick-sliced bread, baked beans,
Semi-skimmed, salt and vinegar crisps,
The Mirror and Dandy comic,
A Fab and a Solero,
At the till with my £20,
Wait for my change,
Ready to go home,
Put my shopping in the bag,
Get home and unpack,
Sit down with my comic and sweets.
I deserve my treat!

Leszek Ujma (11)
Littlegreen School

TWO BIRDS EXPLORING

Over the hill, a distance away
We've got to admit that it's a nice day.
In the woods the trees are swaying,
In the fields, children are playing.
Swoop down to the village, through the streets,
Into the church, people in their seats,
Up through the tower, the bells are ringing,
At the front, the choir is singing.
Out of the church, up to the sky,
Rising above the clouds so high,
It's starting to rain, my feathers are dripping,
It feels like my wings are tipping.
Towards the box and into the nest,
I'm feeling tired and need a rest.

Karl Day (12)
Littlegreen School

OWLS

Feathery ball perched on a tree,
Pointed, twitching ears listening for prey,
Staring with glowing golf ball eyes,
Sharp talons scratching at the branch.

Swooping, diving, grabbing his meal,
Small shadow creatures scramble away.
Returns to his nest with the dead mouse,
Rips the flesh into pieces and feeds it to his young.
Night is drawing to an end
As his eyelids drop and sleep prepares him
For his next evening's work.

James Gatfield (11)
Littlegreen School

RUNNING

The mirror shows a nervous face,
It's the morning of the race,
But who will help me this morning?

I can't stop the chattering of my teeth
As I travel to Broadbridge Heath.
Is there anyone who can help me?

Now I'm lining up just about to start,
All I can feel is the beating of my heart.
But who will help me?

As the man says to get ready,
All I can think of is to take it steady.
Is there anyone who can help me?

As we set off around the track,
All I can feel is people on my back,
But none of those will help me!

It won't be long before the end,
As I come round the final bend,
There's no one now who will help me!

I'm crossing the line and beating the rest,
I've now proved that I am the best.
It's only myself who could help me.

Ryan Breach (12)
Littlegreen School

SWIMMING POOL

People shouting, splashing, having fun.
Jumping, floating, diving under water, doing flips.
Children swimming up and down,
Playing at sharks and crocodiles.
Water splurging out of the side of the pool,
Being swallowed, coughing as they drink.
People walking by the side of the pool,
Falling over, hurting themselves.
Little babies crying, adults laughing,
Children wearing funny frog goggles.
All colours of swimming hats:
Pink, red, yellow, black, green, blue and orange.
The bell goes, the lifeguard shouts,
'All out, time to get out, please.'
People go to get dry and get dressed,
Then home to have a nice up of tea,
And a little nap.

Shane Marshall (12)
Littlegreen School

JESS

Prowling after bird and mouse,
All around the silent house,
This poor old cat is slowly dying,
All the members of the house are crying.

She's started eating less and less,
This poor old cat, her name is Jess.
Silent, fluffy, furry and soft,
Creeping upwards, up to the loft.

Now she looks all grey and thin,
A flea starts biting her flaky skin.
Jess starts dreaming of when she was one,
Rough and tumble and having fun.

Quietly snorting, dreaming on and on,
This poor old cat's life has now all gone.

Wayne Edwards (11)
Littlegreen School

THE JOURNEY

Speeding away from the bank
With the money,
Crash!
All I see is a red light.

Then a strange creature,
With a furry body,
Half-closed eyes
And only three feet tall,
Puts a spell on me.

I feel myself falling,
I hear the sound of bubbling lava,
I smell the rotting flesh of dead people,
I must be at the gates of hell.

Shivering with fear, I enter an enormous hall
With a mighty red figure with horns,
Bloodshot eyes and white, gleaming teeth.
'Bring him to me,' it said.
I was now his slave forever.

Tom Stevens (11)
Littlegreen School

HOLIDAY FUN

I flew to Spain,
Hot dinner on the plane,
Land at eleven,
A very dark heaven,
But the landing lights are bright,
They make me lose my sight.

Finally at my hotel bed,
'Get some sleep,' my mum said.
The sun poured in at half-past eight,
Jumped out of bed, I don't want to be late.

Now I needed to be cool,
So I jumped into the pool,
It was blue, it was cold,
It was great, it was gold.
I went on the bus hopping,
Then I went shopping.

Next day, before dark,
I went to a theme park,
And then it was dinner,
Cheeseburgers make you thinner.
Got to home
And we flew over Rome.

Matt Batchelor (11)
Littlegreen School

WHY?

Hungry,
Deprived,
What have they done?
Nothing.
Walking for miles,
Nothing to drink,
What have they done?
Nothing.
A child's blistered feet,
She's been walking away,
Walking away from what?
Everything.
A weeping mother,
Her children cry because they're starving,
Why?

Because one group, one party, one dictatorship,
Who decided one day
To destroy one city, one country,
To kill the innocent.
Why?
To put one point across,
One point of hate, anger and pure evil.
Why can't they talk it over? Why can't they be calm?
But then why can't there be peace?
Peace between everyone.
But in reality,
Nothing is peaceful.
In the end, war is apparently the only answer.

So, they'll have to keep on walking,
Fleeing from their country.

Amélie Desbiens (13)
Millais School For Girls

TERROR FROM THE SKIES

Another working day dawns in Manhattan,
Smart-suited businessmen like busy ants
Briskly moving towards the towers,
Twin Towers of concrete,
The showpiece of a dramatic skyline.

Suddenly the world seems to stop,
Dumbstruck onlookers witness and explosion,
Like a child's model plane out of control,
It slams with suicidal intent into the tower.

Sirens break the eerie silence of disbelief,
Bewildered workers stand transfixed to the spot,
Raging fire and smoke billow skyward,
Like a hungry dragon consuming all in its path.

Terrified workers leap to certain death,
Escaping the blazing inferno,
Courageous rescue workers evacuate
The once prestigious towers.

Minutes seem like hours,
The streets echo with a bloodcurdling rumble
As the vertical structure disintegrates,
A giant man-made monster,
Collapsing in a pile of dust and smoke,
Like a discarded toy.

Witnesses of the carnage
Run for their lives,
Chased swiftly by clouds of swirling dust,
Choking all in its path, blackening the sky.

All that remains is a twisted skeleton,
Like a horrific monument to the dead.

Will life ever be the same again?

Rosanna Morgan (13)
Millais School For Girls

?

What was it that started as a 'bang'
That killed the people
And damaged the buildings?

What was it that looked like a mushroom,
Oranges, reds and browns,
And that no one could predict?

What was it that destroyed the peace,
That started the hatred
And the tears?

What was it that made the headlines,
That started the hunger
And that made people homeless?

What was it that ended the world?

Claire Allen (13)
Millais School For Girls

MEMORY

I close my eyes
And look to the sky,
Hazy blue with gold sunshine - a beautiful day.

I close my eyes
And see houses, all shapes and sizes
Rising high and awash with vibrant colours.

I close my eyes
And see the park, full of people,
Laughing boldly and running wild.

I close my eyes
And see radios, TVs, my family,
Blaring out, dramatic, joking and nagging.

I close my eyes
And see a world
Of loving comfort, beauty and peace.

I open my eyes
And look to the sky,
Grey and menacing - not a trace of light.

I open my eyes
And see houses, all shapes and sizes,
Derelict in ruins, blackened and charred.

I open my eyes
And see the park, full of people,
Whimpering softly and lying petrified.

I open my eyes
And see radios, TVs, my family,
Blown to pieces, lifeless, in graves.

I open my eyes
And see a world
Of angst, repulsiveness and war.

Tamsin Davison (13)
Millais School For Girls

SEPTEMBER THE ELEVENTH

On September the eleventh,
An incident occurred
That not only shocked America,
It affected the whole world.

Even through they've fallen,
The buildings are replaced,
And however hard it is,
Consequences must be faced.

But when the smoke has cleared
And the ashes swept away,
Who'll pick up the pieces
Of the lives shattered that day?

Julia Rose (14)
Millais School For Girls

MYSTERIOUS WHISPERS

All alone she walked,
The sea spray stinging her face like salty tears.
The gloomy grey sky fell down to the sea,
A strange whisper she heard in her ears.

Almost in a dream she huddles against the wind,
As waves clawed at the shore.
She felt the pull of the sea,
'Is someone calling me?'
the voices whispered once more.

She turned and looked,
No on was there, it was then she noticed the cave.
A cold shudder shot through her body,
Had she found someone's grave?

A strange sparkle caught her eye,
It was a spiral shell glinting on the stones.
With a trembling hand she touched the shell,
As a voice whispered, 'Find my bones.'

In a trance, she stumbled towards the cave,
The sea still grabbing her back.
Inside the darkness filled her eyes,
And a rock behind her clapped.

The mysterious whisper, 'Now you're trapped!'

Nicola Titterrell (12)
Millais School For Girls

LIBRANS

Librans are refined, gentle, affection, we are.
Delicate, diplomatic, dedicated, deep.
Our season's autumn,
When the ploughed earth is resting,
Awaiting next year's seeds.
We are like diamonds, indestructible.

I believe in
Equality, harmony, justice, social order.
Our gods are Venus and Aphrodite,
The goddesses of love.
We are cold,
But afternoons are mild still.

Sally-Ann Hill (11)
Oakmeeds Community College

STARS

Sparkly stars shining
In your eyes,
Like the sun.

What will happen next?
Will they change shape
Or float away?

Will they all vanish
And never come back?

Helen Ahier (11)
Oakmeeds Community College

A SCHOOL DAY

I got up out of bed
        tired.

I walked to school with friends,
        excited.

I saw everyone,
        nervous.

I felt like an ant,
        small.

At break there was running, ranting and raving,
        noisy.

Lunchtime arrived,
        hungry.

We had our first assembly,
        bored.

It was time for home,
        tired again.

Michael Poole (11)
Oakmeeds Community College

AUTUMN LIFE

The trees' crispy hair blowing everywhere,
The breath of a tree produces a gentle breeze,
The sky gets cut and sends down tears,
To a bare-armed child below.

The man of autumn is still young,
As the bright face of the sky matures,
A child stands swaying, with each breath of a tree,
Watching the trees' fingers go bare.

The life of autumn will soon end,
The life of the day gets shorter,
As the trees' hair falls and dances,
Winter waits to come.

Claire Ellis (12)
Oakmeeds Community College

I AM . . .

I am orange,
Vibrant, bright,
Shining like the sun.
On a cool summer morn, there's me,
Floating along on a light summer's breeze.

I am a cat,
The sleek and silent predator,
Affectionate and loyal.
Gone
In the blink of an eye.

I am football,
Fast and furious,
Speeding down the right wing,
There's me scoring,
My team celebrating.

I am me,
Flesh and bones.
What am I?
Feelings and emotions
And the people and things I love.

Stephanie Combe (14)
Oakmeeds Community College

FLAPJACKS

The meowing of the cat sounded as loud as a class of kids,
As we made something that smelled
Sweeter than chocolate.

They were hot as a boiled kettle,
We piled them up just like a pyramid
And they tasted like chocolate pudding.

As the cat licked up the dropped chocolate,
He was purring, as quiet as a whisper.

Hannah Lathwell (11)
Oakmeeds Community College

AUTUMN

Autumn, autumn, the slowest time,
While leaves drop and make a big pile,
Squirrels play and jump all day,
While hedgehogs and badgers bury in the hay.
Short days, long nights
And many a conker fight.
Wild winds pass through skeletons of trees,
So hurry up autumn and pass by, please.

Aled Hancock (11)
Oakmeeds Community College

BELIEF IN THE TWELVE

Twelve constellation creations,
Twelve magical meanings,
Each shared by many people,
Some believe, some don't.

Is it true
Or is it fake?
The shapes formed by shiny stars,
Do they really foretell destiny?

Sammy Jolley (11)
Oakmeeds Community College

ZODIAC

Aquarius, Pisces and Taurus too,
There's twelve altogether of these signs.
Gemini, Cancer and not forgetting Leo,
Six gone so far, let's start the rest.
Finally arriving at Libra and Scorpio,
But coming to the end,
We've got Sagittarius and Capricorn.

Claire Mallows (11)
Oakmeeds Community College

MAN U

Man U is my favourite team,
Giggs is my favourite player,
I like watching Man U on TV,
Giggs dribbles around the players.
I get excited watching Man U,
I like Giggs scoring goals and
Man U getting the cup.

Daniel Beard
Oakmeeds Community College

FUTURE WORLD

More people living on Mars,
More knowledge of the stars,
The cities getting busier,
The world getting bigger,
Aliens flying in the sky,
Weird people with three eyes.
Nobody knows what cars are,
Because everyone goes to the stars.

Hannah Riddleston (11)
Oakmeeds Community College

TO AUTUMN

I called him Russell, like the sound
Of the leaves blowing down the dusty lane.
His hair was matted, like long, damp grass.
He had hazel eyes like the nuts from the trees,
He was tall and thin like a twig.
His lips looked berry red against
His white-stubbled chin, which looked like frost.
He slept like a dormouse from dusk to dawn.

Thomas Grimes (11)
Oakmeeds Community College

SEASONS

The spring brings us flowers
And the grass starts to grow.

The summer gives us hot days,
The summer gives us joy.

The autumn gives us cold days
And people wrap up warm.

The winter gives us snow
And gives us Christmas trees.

Charlotte Woodward (11)
Oakmeeds Community College

AUTUMN

The yellow, red and brown hats are falling off the chocolate branches,
The eyelashes of a woman are turning bright green,
The tears from people start falling down,
The smile of a woman is disappearing behind the black clouds,
The lovely dress on a lovely lady, swaying side to side.

Jessica Zmak (11)
Oakmeeds Community College

BUZZY BEEZ

I'm buzzing in the air
With my fuzzy hair,
Collecting lots of money,
It's always sunny
In my tummy.
I'm buzzing from above
To see my bumble love.

Jacqui Taylor (11)
Oakmeeds Community College

THE HUNTER

As the cat stalks
The silent night,
It swiftly moves
Through the forest,
Looking for prey
To feed its young
To allow them to survive
Their bone-crunching lives.
As the cubs grow
Huge and strong,
The mother slowly fades away
Into the dark depths of the shade.
The cubs grow wise
And catch their own prey,
And remember their mother
On that summer's day.

Jamie Hillwood (11)
Oakmeeds Community College

THE ZODIAC

Is the zodiac about things of the past or future?
Things that might happen now,
Or just another lie coming from someone's mouth,
Or has someone witnessed one person being like that?
Or an astronomer's guess for being
Realistically related revolutionary people
Always act in a way to suit them?

Timmy Gedin (12)
Oakmeeds Community College

ME

Golden sunrays,
Beating down on the crystal, clear, blue sea,
The weather sunny and hot,
Memories of past holidays.

My colour blue,
As deep as the ocean and silky smooth,
Eternal rich sapphire skies,
Cool, calming.

Summer athletics,
Javelin, 'Citius, Altius, Fortius',
Representing Brighton and Hove,
Chanting and cheering in the stadium.

Winter sports,
Netball and hockey, through wind, rain and snow,
Crisp air tearing throats, numbing toes,
Team determination burning through.

Italian food,
Melted butter caught in steaming pasta shells,
Plump tomatoes, scented olives, cracked black peppercorns,
Pizza and pasta.

Man's best friend,
Loyal and loving, totally trusting,
Asking nothing, giving everything,
My best friend.

Meggie Whaley (15)
Oakmeeds Community College

ZODIAC STAR SIGNS

Aquarius is honest and helpful,
Pisces is sensitive and kind,
Aries is confident and quick,
Taurus is placid and patient,
Gemini is youthful and witty,
Cancer is shrewd and protective,
Leo is loving and likeable,
Virgo is diligent and shy,
Libra, charming and urbane,
Scorpio passionate and polite,
Sagittarius, intellectual and fun,
Capricorn, practical and playful.
I don't believe in any of these.
Do you?

Anna Harper (11)
Oakmeeds Community College

THE HURRICANE

No one can predict it,
It's not even in the stars,
It will bring anger and fury,
Before you know it, it's all gone wrong.
It sucks up all the good things
And leaves all the bad things behind,
It's unstoppable in its will,
No one will defeat it.
It tears up all the
Towns, villages
And cities.

Natalia James (11)
Oakmeeds Community College

FANTASTIC FUTURE

Will it be
Calm and peaceful,
As wonderful as wildlife,
Deadly?

Will it be
As frightening as war,
As funny as a comedian,
Or peaceful?

Will it be
Full of happiness, laughter
And glory?

Or will it be
Full of loneliness, sadness
And disappointment?

Nicola Ridley (11)
Oakmeeds Community College

ZODIAC

The zodiac,
Aquarius, Pisces, Aries,
All a star sing wonder,
Cancer, Gemini and Virgo,
Diligent and shy like a mouse,
Sensitive and secretive,
A worrier.
Is it actually true,
Or is it all just a realistic dream?

James Keates (11)
Oakmeeds Community College

My Earliest Memory

As I lay in my cot on a hot summer's evening,
I hungered for water like the hawk hungers for its prey,
Tears streamed down my face like a dying river,
The heat on my skin burned like lava from a volcano.
I wailed like the screams you hear from forgotten ghosts
And my brother across the room slept like a sleeping tiger
in its den.
The peppermint from my teddy bear swirled and flew up into
my nostrils.
I scented it and my tears stopped.
I laid down in my cot and tried to fall back asleep,
But the heat under my skin was killing me.
Then I heard the thud of somebody coming up the stairs,
The great door opened and light flew in like a golden phoenix,
Shattering the darkness like a china plate when it falls and smashes
into a thousand pieces.

Ben Ingram (11)
Oakmeeds Community College

The Life Of A Dragon

The giant red dragon skulks inside his mountain palace,
As he lies on his mountain of gleaming treasure,
Like a hen sitting on her eggs.
The gems sink into his scaly skin,
Making rainbow-coloured armour.
For thousands of years, this beast will wait
For a warrior to kill him for his treasure.
Sadly, in this new age, the dragon does not exist.

Jason Dela Nougerede (11)
Oakmeeds Community College

I AM A SUNFLOWER

I am a golden sunflower,
Swaying in the summer breeze,
My delicate yellow petals
Surround my fragile seeds.

Summer is the season that I grow,
Basking in the long-awaited heat,
My roots plunge deep into the earth,
My head turns towards the sky.

I grow until the autumn comes,
When my golden petals fall.
The winter frost will soon begin
And snow will coat the ground.

But spring will come around in time
And my seeds will start to climb.

Victoria Riddleston (14)
Oakmeeds Community College

THE FUTURE

The future, it's coming, it's closer and closer,
Every second, minute, day and night.
It's in with the new and out with the old.
Every day we dream of the future,
Will we have floating cars floating like bumblebees
Or find aliens short and green?
We will never know, but how we wish.
What will it be like in the future.
The future I don't know about, do you?

Siobhan Hancock (12)
Oakmeeds Community College

WINTER

I am the sea, the blue, crystal-clear
Waters that shine like winter icicles.

I am a rose that lets petals fall,
It brings you happiness, the deep red colour
Like a warm smile.

I am a droplet of snow
Who brings joy to people's winters.

I am a horse that gallops freely
Through the fields.

I am the sea, the waves, they make you relax
And forget your troubles and fears.

Grace Hill (14)
Oakmeeds Community College

THE ERUPTION

The volcano blew,
The town ran,
Everyone was scared
Of the red, fiery ash
Running down the hill,
Like a fierce avalanche,
Spitting and blowing.
Stops, suddenly silent
All around
Except for one sound,
That was the eruption.

Joshua Reeve (11)
Oakmeeds Community College

AUTUMN

The hair swaying brassy blonde of the
Dancing female, dancing with the wind.
The rain dripping slowly down her fingertips,
Brown, yellowy-golden dress reflects the autumn sun.

Yellow and brown twinkles on the green ivory dress,
Bare skin showing through the ivory dress,
Ghostly white face, glowing through the
Darkness of the coat.

The coloured hair of a girl
Makes a curved line in the darkened background.

Hannah Denyer (11)
Oakmeeds Community College

AUTUMN HAS ARRIVED

Winds whipping through the branches,
Leaves falling like locks of curly hair.
Browns, greens, reds,
Caught in a multicoloured twister.
Autumn has arrived.

Conkers waiting to be picked from the ground,
Like a box of chocolates waiting to be eaten.
Sycamore seeds dancing in the breeze,
Like a ballerina swirling, twirling around on the stage.
Autumn has arrived.

Devon Busby (11)
Oakmeeds Community College

AUTUMN IN THE FUTURE

Autumn as it is today,
The leaves fall down and start to play,
The branches start to lose their hair
And the clouds begin to burst.

But think about the future to come
And how the summer says it's done,
Then the autumn steps on stage
And starts to play the part.

The leaves don't fall,
The winds don't blow,
The grass doesn't 'Mexican Wave' any more,
Because we are in the future, everything has changed.

But just because we're in the future,
It doesn't mean to say that spring and summer,
Autumn and winter, won't come out to play.

Stephanie Brown (12)
Oakmeeds Community College

SCORPION

Scorpion,
Powerful,
Deadly,
A great enemy of tarantula,
Like an evolved
Form of a crab.
The desert is its habitat,
Like a prisoner to it,
Trapped with tarantulas,
A never-ending battle.

Tom Whitworth (11)
Oakmeeds Community College

MY EARLIEST MEMORIES

My grandad's old tweed jacket,
Like dry, chequered fields in the summer,
A chequer board with history as long as time.
His armchair, where we both sat,
Red as an early crimson morning, before it rains.
Big as a volcano, pulling me in,
Soft as a Persian cat, entwining its fur around my body.

The orange Tango we drank,
Like a flood of fizzy orange, bubbling over my tastebuds,
Numbing my tongue.
The Minirolls and Jaffa Cakes we ate,
Like tasting forbidden chocolate from Mr Wonka's factory,
Sticking to my teeth like superglue.

The smell of chocolate,
Like being in a chocolate orchard.
The pipe tobacco he smoked,
Choking me then neutralising my lungs like anaesthetic,
Musty cobwebs
Irritating my nose, making me sneeze like someone allergic
                                        to a dog.

My dad's shoes,
Stamping along the hall like a giant.
The sound of Nana and Mum chatting,
Like a receptionist in a US sitcom, not doing any work.
Moggy, purring in Grandad's arms,
Like an earthquake about to break out.
All the sounds combining
Like the M25 on a Bank Holiday Monday.

Laura Jupp (12)
Oakmeeds Community College

TIME

Some people are funny people,
Because they always ask the time,
But they will never know the mite.
Mite, you ask? You do not know.
If you rearrange the letters
You'll know what I mean!

Tim Cooper (11)
Oakmeeds Community College

WALKING HOME IN THE DARK

Dancing flames
Far away in distance
Fading spirit
Snowy owls
Hooting vowels
Silhouetted trees
Bright moonlight
Jet-black shadows
Dark grey road
Bitter air
Sweaty hair
Dry eyes
Blazing bonfire
Stony gravestones
Looking sacred
Enchanting air
Reeking beer
Dancing flames
Far away.

Taimoor Cheema (12)
Oathall Community College

AN AFGHAN CHILD

Away over rusty mountains, stroking the sky,
A place where my homeland and happy thoughts lie.
Away from the terror, the suffering and all,
Alone in a world in which I feel so small.

Over high mountains, over lone plain,
Oh will I ever see my home again?
Or will it become a nightmare of war,
Please somebody tell me, what's it all for?

Across rocky ground, stones pricking my feet,
There's nowhere to stay, there's little to eat.
The crops would just die, there's no fields to mow,
But we'll keep on going, though the pace is slow.

Around me is a world, so empty and bare,
There's dust on my heart, there's dust everywhere.
The day is so hot, I feel so tired and lost,
The night is so bitter, the cold and the frost.

I feel like an ant amongst buildings high,
Stuck between desert and pastel blue sky.
The sun watches over us, travelling slow.
What's the point? I so want to know.

Fear of the bombs, the pain and the war,
But we keep on walking though our feet are sore.
My mum's covered up, hiding behind a cloth screen,
For no one to see - our leader's regime.

But still back there, is my cosy warm home,
I never felt so hungry, so tired or alone.
Away, far away from impending fight,
We'll follow our hearts, we'll follow the light.

Emma Musson (12)
Oathall Community College

STEPPING COLOURS

I step into my mind.
All around are swirling colours of creativity and imagination,
I jump back as a spark of thought races past me.
Now I begin to look past the colours and sparks to a dark world.
There are no colours there.
All I can see are dark thunderclouds full of black thoughts.
I venture further.
I walk away from the colours and into the dark, bleak world.
This place is only black and grey,
Its bareness is more than I can take.
I try to get back to the colours, but I'm trapped.
A wall of darkness has closed up behind me.
Is there no way out?
I stare into the misery.
Is that a small puddle reflecting the light from the coloured world,
                                        or is it my exit?
Picking up a stone, I throw it into the pool of light,
There is no splash,
I take a risk and jump.
Mixtures of colours are flying past.
I am falling, falling,
Then with a soft thud, I land on the bouncy floor of the world of
                                        colours once more.

Emily Stiles (12)
Oathall Community College

RED ROSE

Red rose in the sun,
Glistening bright with real beauty,
Save me from my fate.

From white-winged moth,
Carrying a pure white rose bud
As pure as the snow.

Happy in my heart,
As clear as a bright sunset,
Over the hillside.

The red rose tonight
Filled my heart with love tonight,
Warm as a petal.

Lucy Smith (11)
Oathall Community College

THE CONDOR

She flies above the mountains,
Where no man has ever been,
Ducking and diving, catching the currents,
Then soars over the seas.

She perches a minute to get her breath,
Then sets off to rule the sky,
The condor is the leader
Over the mountains high.

The waves of the wind
Run through her feathers,
Catching thermals
Under cumulus clouds.

As she glides through the air
With no care in the world,
Her fluffy white ruff
And eagle-like stare.

Free and wild,
Circling around,
No one to tame her
So far from the ground.

Michael Marchant (12)
Oathall Community College

WISHES AND DREAMS

Dreams are wishes in your mind,
Happy, endless, sad or kind.

Do you close your eyes and go to sleep
And think of fairies and your dreams that they keep?
Or perhaps you've wished on a fairy chant,
Hoping your wishes they will grant.

Or do you believe in a wishing well,
Where your silver goes in and your dreams start to swell?
And the crystal water splutters and gleams,
As if responding and brewing up your dreams.

Or maybe you wish upon a star and find out who you really are.
When the sun goes in and the moon rises high,
And the stars like shattered glass in the sky
Twinkle your thoughts and hopes in your eyes.

You might trust the angels and God above,
To surround and keep you in their endless love.
However you dream, it's up to you
And may your greatest wish come true.

Katie Sommers (12)
Oathall Community College

LIFE SENTENCE

Eternally, left in open field,
Internally, left by the gate of earth,
Completely surrounded, yet all alone
In cover of darkness, yet shrouded in light
A wanderer - it could not be
This stranger in his heart - free.

Geoffrey Allott (12)
Oathall Community College

THE MATCH

Shin pads on, boots laced tight
Today we're going to have a fight.
Put my shirt on, number two,
Feeling nervous, I need the loo!
The pitch looks muddy, the goals are tall,
We'll have some cracks and whack the ball.
Warm-up time, we'll jog, stretch and walk,
Then it's time for the manager's talk.
I take my position behind the defence
And wait for the whistle, feeling tense.
The ref calls the keepers, 'I'm ready to blow.'
The whistle sounds and off we go.
The passes are long, the crosses are good
We're going to win, well, I think we should.
Players approaching, one with the ball.
I put in a tackle, he takes a fall.
I pass the ball forward, right down the wing.
Our striker is on it and he takes a swing.
He hits it hard - his shooting is brill.
What a goal! We're up 1-0!

William Walkinton (11)
Oathall Community College

SPRING

S pectacular flowers bloom in the morning sun,
P erfect lambs bleat as little sparrows fly home,
R ight now an egg is hatching into a little chick,
I n a field a cow is giving birth to a wobbly calf,
N ow it is almost dawn, rabbits speed around, their tails
bobbing rapidly,
G reen leaves fill the trees once more.

Kamella Clough (11)
Oathall Community College

HAMSTER

His eyes are black as coal in sunlight
On a cloudless day,
When he looks out at night
Between the bars,
He looks sad.
His eyes follow you everywhere.

Silky smooth fur,
Smooth as an eyebrow.
He's quiet as a thief,
Or sometimes sniffing like a person
With a cold in the winter.
He sneezed once,
Eyes closed, ears flapping down,
Like he was sleeping for a second.

Fibre optic whiskers
Twitch separately
Like a spider's legs.
His claws like a digger
Can rip like a tiger.
As he climbs my hand,
He leaves white scratches
As he slips.

He loves the rustling
Of cereal packets
And the taste of raisins.
Sometimes he's afraid
To come out,
Clings to the bars
As I try to bring him out.
He doesn't like to be rushed.

I don't know what he dreams of,
But I expect he wishes for food
And freedom.

Timothy Russell-Croucher (13)
Oathall Community College

THE BUTTERFLY

The butterfly flutters by,
Attracted to the light
Which is so bright.
It flies up higher,
Like V-Rally
Can you smell
The burning tyre?
It gets in a trap
And makes the noise,
Tap, tap, tap.
It's free at last
It flutters by,
But in the next adventure
Will it die?

Amy Hicks (12)
Oathall Community College

WOLF

I was walking home in the cold, driving rain,
And it was then I heard that cry of pain.
A cry of someone stabbed with a knife,
A cry that was soon to change my life.

I stepped off the road and into the trees,
With a trembling feeling down by my knees.
I turned a corner and there I found,
A man lying dead on the ground.

I looked around and there by a tree,
A grey wolf looked straight back at me,
And slowly dripping from his jaw,
A trail of blood fell to the floor.

The wolf's staring eyes and just beneath,
A mouthful of his sharp white teeth.
A horrible smell, evil and foul,
The wolf let out a bloodcurdling growl.

I reached to my pocket and pulled out a gun,
The wolf stood up and started to run,
But he did not run away behind a tree,
No, he ran straight towards me.

He opened his jaws which could do some harm,
And bit me hard on my right arm.
I made it to the hospital and waited a bit,
All they did was bandage it.

And I still have the scar from that evil bite,
I'm human by day, but werewolf by night.

Oliver Wright (13)
Oathall Community College

CATS

Cats, agile, alert,
Motionless waiting to pounce,
The string shakes, they spring.

Their fur, silky soft,
Nestling, purring on your lap,
Rumbling volcanoes.

Laura Pinfield (13)
Oathall Community College

AUTUMN

Nice sunny day,
Clouds passing by,
Flowers finishing growing by the second.
Sense the smell of scented flowers.
A nice, gentle autumn breeze
And the saying of the trees
And the rustling of the dry leaves.
Rosebuds have lost their petals,
The sunflowers have long gone,
People are busy tidying up.
We are all waiting now for the new year
And springtime to brighten up our days again.

Barry Bastable (14)
Palatine School

HAUNTED HOUSE

In a street
In a house
In a loft
The family hear
Strange noises.

What is that?
A mouse, a rat?
Could it be
A ghost? Let's see!

Oh no! A ghost!
Whoooooo!

Lee Greenfield (13)
Palatine School

RACING CARS

I love racing cars,
Engines revving on the track,
Tyres screeching as they start,
Skids squealing round the corners,
Gears clashing to go faster,
Crowds cheering when they win.

Martin Vickery (13)
Palatine School

PARENTS' SAYINGS

Go and do the dishwasher please,
Go to your room, Daniel, *now!*
Did you have a nice day at school, Daniel?
Go to bed Daniel, please.
Daniel, dinner's ready.
Go and tidy your room now Daniel.
Go and take the dog for a walk.
Go and tidy the kitchen please.
Don't be too long on the phone.
Come in at eight o'clock.
Don't forget to take your phone with you.
Have a nice day at school.
Have you got any homework?
Can you make me a drink, Daniel, please?
Can you put your shoes away?

Daniel Strong (15)
St Anthony's School, Chichester

PARENTS' SAYINGS

Go out to play.
Go and tidy your bedroom.
Go out on your bike.
Go away, go and play with your brothers.
Go and do your homework.
Go and do the washing up.
Go and cook your dinner.

Stephen Mariner (13)
St Anthony's School, Chichester

PARENTS' SAYINGS

Try this on please.
Walk the dog.
Dinner's ready.
Get ready for bed.
Here's your dinner money.
Get ready for school.
Put the animals away.
I'm watching the TV -
What is it now?
See you soon.

Donna Cairns (13)
St Anthony's School, Chichester

ME, MYSELF AND I

My mum said, 'Daniel, have you cleaned your teeth?
Daniel, have you done your homework?
Daniel, dinner is ready.
Daniel, turn your music down low.
Daniel, it's time to get up for school.
What time will you be in tonight?
Be good and get on with your work.
Clean out your guinea pigs and give them clean water.
Daniel, your minibus is here for school.
Please pay attention in class.'

Daniel Playford (13)
St Anthony's School, Chichester

WHAT PARENTS SAY TO YOU

Go and do your homework.
Go to bed.
Stop fighting with your brother.
Go and brush your teeth.
Put your glasses on.
Go and tidy your room.
Get your school stuff ready.
Help me with the washing up.
Turn the music down.
Eat all of your dinner.

Salima Tollaz (12)
St Anthony's School, Chichester

PARENTS' SAYINGS

Go and do your bedroom.
Make your own food if you don't like mine.
You have to take your sister with you.
Go and do your homework.
Hurry up, you will be late for the bus.
Go and walk the dogs.
Go and watch your TV,
It is our time now.
Go and feed the animals.
Don't expect to go back out.

Kelly Tupper (13)
St Anthony's School, Chichester

PARENTS' SAYINGS

Go to your room.
Tidy up your room
Shut up,
Put it away.
Get ready to go to school.
Go to school.
No, put your best clothes on.
Put the video back.
Turn the radio down.
Go and play football.

Dean Shelley (13)
St Anthony's School, Chichester

PARENTS' SAYINGS

Go to bed.
Don't watch your TV, it's very late.
Tidy your room.
Sort out the washing please.
You don't have to come and see me.
Here is your pocket money.
Get your backside up the stairs.
Make your bed.
Tidy your sister's room
And don't upset your brother.

Eva Perks (14)
St Anthony's School, Chichester

PARENTS' SAYINGS

Do your homework.
Get to bed or you won't get up in the morning.
Tidy your room.
Wash your face and teeth.
When did you last wash your feet?
The answer's 'No!'
If you don't like this café, find another one.
Don't mind me, I'm just your mother.
The biscuits are for everyone, OK?
Stop watching TV.

Alastair Reeves (14)
St Anthony's School, Chichester

PARENTS' SAYINGS

You're certainly not putting that on any wall in this house.
Why don't you take the dog for a walk?
Have you cleaned your teeth?
Get off that computer, you've been on it for hours.
You can stop talking, silence is OK sometimes.
Stop chewing on your brace.
Star Trek, aaargh!
Tidy your room. It's a pig sty.
Have you go any homework?
You used to be a lovely baby, and then you grew up!

David Taylor (14)
St Anthony's School, Chichester

PARENTS' SAYINGS

Can you lay the table please?
It is time to turn off the TV.
Put your pyjamas on.
Drink your tea.
Good night - God bless.
Get on with your work.
Do you understand?
Any questions?
It is time to go to bed.
Have you done your homework?

Gina Quest (13)
St Anthony's School, Chichester

PARENTS' SAYINGS

Tidy your bedroom.
Put your clothes away.
Turn your music down.
Stop shouting at me.
Stop fighting.
Get in the bath.
Get to sleep.
Do your homework.
What do you want for your dinner?
Can you water in the greenhouse?

Rebecca Barc (12)
St Anthony's School, Chichester

PARENTS' SAYINGS

Stop talking.
Thank you for your help.
If a job's worth doing, it's worth doing well.
Tidy your room.
No!
Well done.
Have you brushed your hair and had a wash?
Have you made your bed and drawn your curtains?
That's too much make-up.
Can you put your ironing away please.

Beth Quinn (13)
St Anthony's School, Chichester

PARENTS' SAYINGS

Go outside and play.
Go and tidy your room.
Make your own food if you don't like it.
Go and take the dogs on a walk.
If you go out take your brother with you.
You can say goodbye to going out to play.
Can you make me a cup of tea?
Do your homework before going out.
You can stay in for hurting your brother.

Chaz Walter (13)
St Anthony's School, Chichester

Parents' Sayings

Go and make me a cup of coffee.
Go and do the washing up.
Go down to the shop for me.
Can you tidy up a little bit?
You were lovely when you were a little baby.
Can you two stop arguing?
Go and answer the phone.
She always has the last sentence.
You two are like cat and dog.
Make me some toast.

Chamaine Knight (14)
St Anthony's School, Chichester

Parents' Sayings

Go and tidy your bedroom.
Put all your washing in the wash bin.
Go and do your homework.
Do the washing up now.
Stop watching that TV right away.
Go to your bedroom, right now!
Wake up, you have got to go to school.
Come and have your dinner.
Go and have your shower.
Do as you are told.

Chris Smith (14)
St Anthony's School, Chichester

PARENTS' SAYINGS

Take the dog for a walk.
Tidy your room up.
Feed the dog.
Cut the lawn.
Poop-a-scoop.
Make sure the back door is open.
Make sure you clean your teeth.
Make sure you shut the gate.
Make sure you shut the garage door.
Be back for dinner.

Scott Chandler (13)
St Anthony's School, Chichester

PARENTS' SAYINGS

Go and do it.
Can you go down to the shop?
Go to bed.
Get your clothes on.
Eat your breakfast.
Do you want a drink?
Come in, it's raining.
Have you got your PE kit?
We're going out.
Do you want to play now, it might rain later?

Daniel Wilkins (13)
St Anthony's School, Chichester

PARENTS' SAYINGS

Do you want to go to town?
Come on. Out of bed, get your clothes on.
Have you fed your hamsters?
Get your homework done.
Go upstairs, play your music and leave me alone!
Go and get something else on.
That's nice, wear that.
Do you want it in a ponytail, pigtails or plaits?
Give me a twirl.
Eat your potatoes!

Christine Clear (13)
St Anthony's School, Chichester

PARENTS' SAYINGS

Don't be late!
Get up, Louise.
I love you.
Go out to play.
Go to bed.
Feed the cat, Louise.
Don't be late.
Wash up, Louise.
Clean your teeth.

Louise Waller (13)
St Anthony's School, Chichester

UNIDENTIFIED OBJECTS

A brown and white little critter which comes out
At the dead of night.
Smiles which last forever.
Connecting me to others.
Unlocking my way through life.
Ticking which goes on for eternity.
A meeting I can look back on.
Dreaded by all teenagers, but put up with!
Wanted by everyone, used by everyone, earned
By some and begged by others.
Turning helpless humans into couch potatoes
By a flick of a switch.
Savings from long ago to help me learn and grow.

Martin Capon (13)
Sackville Community College

MY LIFE IN A BOX

The sounds of madness within,
Shielded from the outside world,
Sounds of a dream
That one day will definitely be.
Dead wood but, like me, lives for music.
The silent maker of pictures
And memories, my life
Reflected behind glass.
My young days remembered
With a simple gift.
My own bible, guiding me forward,
Inflating me with adrenalin and speed.
My need for light and warmth, given,
Always on time helping me to be.

Jonathan Hallett (15)
Sackville Community College

PERCEPTIONS OF MYSELF

My inner soul, released in notes,
Playing the one true song
That touches my heart,
Ghosts of music hidden away
In another world concealed
Inside imagination,
Waiting to be released
Suddenly
Set free to the universe.

The knowledge of many
Handed down
Through bonds which stretch
Tighter than blood
Feeding my sense of adventure,
My will to learn
And explore.

Thought ignores time,
Feeling its way
Through the puzzles that twist
Inside my mind
And disrupt the concentration
Set on recorded knowledge,
Spreading peace and control
In the confusion
And chaos
And harshness of reality.

In the end
It never matters at all.
My frustration
Taken out on a hollow ball's field
And my humour
Transferred to the real world
Are unimportant,
Non-existent
And like dreams to the future,
Fade away.

Sandy Mill (14)
Sackville Community College

MY FAVOURITES

She was cute, she was cuddly,
She was ginger and white,
My rabbit was my favourite,
But turned into a spirit of the night.
I loved my grandma very much too,
But she turned into a spirit,
Oh boo-hoo!

My guinea pig, Benjy,
Died last week,
I've only got my dad left.
Things are looking bleak.
Then Dad said, 'No more pets for you this week.'
So now I'm looking bleak.

I suppose there's always my brother,
But he is a bit of a pest,
I love him very dearly,
He is the very best.

Sammy Gates (13)
Sackville Community College

I AM THIS COLOUR

I am this colour,
A simple love-hate relationship
Though the other side of the word not forgotten,
A crown of flowers carries more significance
Than a golden ring;
The spiky exterior hides
Treasures of silk, a reminder of being little,
A vinyl burst of pop no longer appreciated,
Graceful, artistic talent,
A gem hopefully inherited,
Comfort so great,
Yet objects so small,
Dangerous habit; smoke and fire
Sliced with scissors,
Shining tendrils fall but soon return,
Impressions cheat the eye,
Glittering things can belong to dull people.
I know,
I am this colour.

Rachel Burrows (15)
Sackville Community College

LIFE IN A SHOE BOX

The words of work and pleasure, becoming merged over time,
But lost by a comforting presence,
Imaginary life in the mind of the young.

Musical mayhem, manipulating feelings and
Visions of faces constantly with you, however distant.
The company of twelve, glistening to bring rewards
Of indulgence wrapped in consequence.

A traditional act to the despair of family,
Later showing problems but with solution, however,
Just around the corner,
Complicated networks of words to carry you closer and,
Although artificial, support is part of life.
The feeling of contentment in this safe haven, there always.

Hannah Mitchell (14)
Sackville Community College

MY LIFE

My own passion being played by professionals,
The hope of winning in a stroke of a kick,
The celebration afterwards, being rewarded,
A sense of achievement, written in the form of words.
Memories that come back through words,
Written by a special friend.
Childhood signatures that are not on paper,
A flame that never burns out, but
Sums up a big occasion in a child's life.
A catch opens, revealing faces who fed me and
Still guide me through life.
A gold snake-like present can be touching,
A place that cannot be replaced even at home,
Cannot be forgotten though.
A gasp of awe, in a motion of a splash,
Captured by a look.
A memory that can be rewound.
My memories are a secret no one knows or understands,
But I do,
And I won't ever forget them.

Sarah Scamell (14)
Sackville Community College

A LOOK AT LIFE

One's life is remembered through fleeting snapshots
Of times and places.
Memories hold elements, portraying my feelings
And hopes.
Flesh and blood nurture me, sustaining important values
Showing loving kindness.
Childhood, a time for gifts of unconditional love,
A special present, safe forever.
A band of gold; a mark of love. Butterflies with no wings
Handle with care, securing a stud of gold.
Friends give gifts of faraway memories,
Printed for posterity.
Time moves on, expectations demand we grow.
The face is a blank canvas awaiting the soul to open.
Caring, an important value. A furry friend
That feeds so much love and affection.
Depending on you for life!
The fashion accessory the world depends on,
Reliving memories, again and again.

Charlotte Busby (13)
Sackville Community College

ADAM

My first step to freedom and
My only memory of part of my parents,
Small wheels that enable me to fly,
An image that disappears and
The experience of a lifetime,
The things that are cuddly to me and my family,
The image of life to me.

Adam Fryer (13)
Sackville Community College

MY LIFE IN A SHOE BOX

The first toy has always been there from the beginning.
First love, in the form of lots of fur and meowing.
My father's influence on me, a reward in life,
And my mother's, my faith and belief.
Me with my mode of transport, not a car, but as good to me.
The addiction, the only way I can escape this world
Into entertainment.
Me, with my one contact with a friend when I feel alone,
Despite all this, one still remains,
The one that is always there for me in work or play,
And one who has left me with a sharp and painful memory.
Now all that's left is the one thing which I need to rub out
The bad memories to fill them with happy ones.

Luke Johnson (14)
Sackville Community College

MY SHOE BOX POEM

Headlines from the start of time are
Influencing me through words for
My life is written out before me.
The key to friendship
Is the first possession in life.
Friends and foe united in a portfolio of existence
Forever engraved in stone.
Friends at your fingertips are
The award for years of hard work.

Barry Southwell (14)
Sackville Community College

MYSELF

A shining silver which glides me through air,
Whilst carefully watching upon the pace of hands.
I look at a gloss from which I am afar,
But I know the real thing will always mean care.
What seeks in my pocket, I use its power, a dare.
It is this that I turn to unlock my movement,
My sounds I hear for my personal rock.
I shall look to the pages for thorough improvement
For the race of graphics I power such pace,
I look at things.
A card which was sent by me and a face
Of which I know, friendly and best,
When finally I finish to put movement in a lock.

Andrew Coghill (14)
Sackville Community College

MY REALITY

Those first few steps unravel the miracle of mankind,
The grey box in the corner of the room
That takes away the boredom, from
This place of knowledge I'm stuck with,
I look at my reflection to put on my fake face,
An individual image or maybe not,
A chain of friendship reminds me of those fond memories,
Communicating with letters rather than speech,
My favourite club heard as I reach for the stars,
And those lookalikes that I cherish,
Gave a sign of love and maturity.

Charlotte Nisbet (13)
Sackville Community College

ME

A sweet, fluffy bundle, warm and soft,
Reminds me of my first day,
My collective obsession, metal and shiny,
Imaginative thoughts, enchanted dreams,
As I flick through the magical pages,
Smiling faces, gleaming looks,
Bring a smile to my face,
Simple and organised, my own experience,
Emerald green and a band of silver
For a special day.
Legs trampling down the highway,
My very special gift, though not making up
For the memory of past, painful
And special which lies alive forever.

Sasha Crossley (13)
Sackville Community College

SEAN'S PLEASURES

I rely on a line with the wind blowing into my face,
My memory is made up of mega bites.
My eyes were surrounded by words,
Small knives gripping into the ground
Enabling me to accelerate.
They keep me company when I am alone.
The devils believe in a team sport,
I always rely on smiles which gradually fade away.
Without it, I would never remember dream land,
It was just finished in a flash.

Sean Wilson-Agate (13)
Sackville Community College

SECRET ADDRESS

My box of memories is taking me on a journey,
The journey of my life so far.
My struggle for excellence is rewarded by a bit of paper
Which will take me to the future.
My need for speed at a blink of an eye
Whilst watching the screen in an intense manner.
Lots of work and operations helping me to get my smile,
My musical obsession, sounding graceful in the air.
A photographic image of the present day and a
Photographic past that will be remembered.
My way of relaxing whilst watching the screen,
My potting obsession bringing me metal sculptures
Again and again,
My travelling around the world taking me up and down,
Then the lid closes.

Michael Bowes (13)
Sackville Community College

MY LIFE IN A SHOE BOX

My mind on paper, thoughts are visible,
Never late, ever early, recording every second.
Instant communication at the touch of a button,
The start of a life, the ability to read,
The power of laughter.
A token from almost every country in the world,
A cherished memory from years past.
The power of music that only you can hear.
Faces from every day, yet different.
A friend who's always there.

Andrew Smith (13)
Sackville Community College

MEMORIES

A key to another place,
Letting me escape for my independence,
Clearing my mind of troubles and feelings,
Into the form of words,
My loving comfort to remain in my arms,
Always around to cuddle and care for.
All fluffy and soft to lay in my lap,
So far away, but close in my heart
Enabling me to remember my
Infantile efforts,
Entertainment and ability,
Names of identity still with me
From the past,
A present and memory
Reminding me of who I am.
Gazing into a frame,
Gone in time, but still loved.

Emma Hughes (13)
Sackville Community College

MY WORLD

Something I can hear when I'm not in gear,
When it's all quiet, I put on a riot,
A remembrance of football is all I need,
The proof of a match that I have seen,
A small, magical world controlled by my hands,
It's from across the water, but hung around my neck,
It goes as fast as you want, but a bit small for a ride,
With this little gadget I can do stunts with my fingers,
With this, I can catch a dish.

Shaun Hammond (13)
Sackville Community College

NEVER FORGOTTEN

The Great One's creation not yet in this world,
The miracle of life binds us
Together for life, until darkness shall fall.
Her face, her lovingness in the form of a smile,
The joy of a precious gift held in his arms,
Pretty and natural images of life formed in lines.
The colour of bronze, an achievement.
Beyond this world, the stars I look,
Knowing peace is upon him.
Careful treatment, big change of movement,
Circle of gold in my hand reminds me of her.
Sweet gift from the past brings fresh memories to my head.
I stand and remember, thoughts flood back.
Never forgotten.

Stacey Telford (14)
Sackville Community College

SILENT PLACE

The silent round thing, which gets anything,
It is quite old and has a big fold,
You can take place in a race,
It is all soft, stuck in the loft.
I can see what is next to me,
It is card, but not very hard.
Something from under, you're done if you blunder,
Listening for quaint sounds of life,
Through air space, from place to place
You can move without touching the ground.

Oliver Benwell (14)
Sackville Community College

SCOTT'S POEM

The need for light in the dark,
With that precious gift for the occasional drink
Makes my heart grow.
The way I enter through things.
In the dark it reminds me of that soft, cuddly object
That will always be in my heart.
My education, fun and imagination gives me what I need.
My frame of love that reminds me of my life
And family, wherever I may be.
That soft, warm object dries me when I get out of the water
After that amazing encounter with those beautiful creatures.
That ring and connect-up make my life more interesting.
That solid gold object hangs round my neck
To make me feel good and important.
My sport gives me what I need, something to protect my
Mouth in that short moment of contact.

Scott Goble (13)
Sackville Community College

THE POEM ON MY LIFE

This kept me snug and warm through the night.
He is soft, furry and warm and keeps me company.
It came out with ease.
Snip! Snip! And away it went.
The memories shoot back to me when I see it again.
It is on day and night, giving me information about the world.
This keeps me and others occupied through the long hours of the day.
My small, feathery friend.
The memory which will last forever.

David Perry (13)
Sackville Community College

MY FINAL DRAFT

I'm the origin of all things, shelter for creation,
With strings that weave in six
Or music will never sound the same.
'Are you the Eggman?' 'We are the Eggmen.'
'I am the walrus, and this is the ultimate test.'

Many things have been proved, but how to justify life?
Laughter. Pure and innocent. All
Mastered within this roll of film
This may seen square and simple,
Yet most would never complete its winding voyage.

It's a game of bat and ball. Hollow inside,
However flies at the pace of light.
It won't be easy.
(But nothing is!)

Time stacks up, tension grows,
Then all fades away - to emptiness.
. . . I am not there yet.

'After all, success is not a statistic,
It's a passion,' as the wise man says.
Celebrate sportsmanship! Fly if you can
And trail behind the cheers/jeers.

Time has flown by . . .

I will treasure the ticket that allows me to teleport
Back to my friends, lost in the wilderness.
'And as the wheels slow ever further, crystals of snow
will engrave me, leaving nothing, lest a heavy shell
in the midst of winter.'

Chao Yu (15)
Sackville Community College

NEVER-ENDING MEMORIES

As I journey through my life and loves
My thoughts and feelings divine, trapped
In a circle of sterling silver like half
Of a whole, circles, linked together forming
The strength of friendship as I stare eye
To eye at the faces that I love even
Though I talk and I laugh, my friend I
Cannot see, you may be miles away
And still be near.

Stuck in a box with two walls and two
Ceilings, not seeing enough of the amazing
Outside world that surrounds me,
It matters not what they say, the inside
Of you is by far more beautiful It's glow
Is more spectacular than the early morning
Sunrise, it shines as the sign of innocence,
So small, yet such an achievement.
You ask, yet how else could I express myself,
Other than pages and pages of lifetime memories.

The paper decorations to some another language,
But to me, my way of forming beautiful sounds
As the disc, helps me to surf through
The waves of sound and the journey of eternity.

Rachael Charles (13)
Sackville Community College

LIFE IS A MEMORY

Protecting the past,
Unlocking the future,
Galloping images
Racing through time,
Dancing to victory,
Lasting forever,
Written words of the past
Creating a smile,
Speeding through waters,
To silver on string,
Blooming life
To strengthen the weak,
A bundle of memories
Close to the heart,
The smile of my influence
Protecting the meek,
Placid in a picture,
Moving in memory,
A loop of love
From the influence of time,
For life is a memory
For each individual,
But this special memory's
Entirely mine.

Suzi Hoare (13)
Sackville Community College

ALWAYS

Their faces will always remind me,
Helping me, being there for me, stronger than a rock
And as a symbol of my past, all I know and belongs
To me, I wear around my neck.
Alongside that, as a reminder of myself and my beliefs,
Strong, hang a chain of silver that connects us all.
If I ever want to escape, I can.
I can fly into a different world.
I can feel and sense, I am not me anymore.
My fondest memories of my early life, my imagination,
The colours and light exploding from my own hands.
Even then I shared everything,
The laughs, the tears, the fun we've had, without
Them I could not be, I can keep this as a memory
And this decorative piece of paper, a reminder that
With a touch of my fingers, sweet-sounding music
Can engulf the surroundings.
Yet I wouldn't be able to without her,
Influencing me always, the founder of my skill.
Stretching my ability, she still remembers.
Wherever I go, I can see them,
So soft to touch, they are my listeners.

Sarah Evans (13)
Sackville Community College

MEMORIES

Although I cannot see you, the memories remain
Close to me, in my heart and in my soul.
Small childish words keep you close to my love
Sent from God above.
There are trapped memories that remain forever
In a silver band that lights up my life
In the middle of the dark.
My comfort from birth keeps me warm at night,
Good memories remain in the softness of the dark.

The arch of freedom in childhood memories,
Trapped in a silver band.
A swirl of colourful beads brought upon me
Once among golden sands.
Small memories, tiny babies all around
My room are treasured forever.
United colours clash, shoulder to shoulder,
Washed of mud and fury.
All these memories are close to my heart
And nothing will tear them apart.
A chain of memories on a circle of friendship,
Which will go on at a very high speed.

Jenna Knott (13)
Sackville Community College

LEARNING

My identity printed to never fade,
Insignificant so long ago,
It grows stronger every year.
The loveable creature reminding me of my childhood,
Our soft bundle we loved so much,
Wearing the belt, we knew he was secure.
With the welcome sign into my world,
Teaching me what he needed me to know.
I wear the memory of my old friends,
Frozen in time forever.
The small farm of education,
Teaching me the importance of my future.
With my safe way to know
I can reach those most important to me.
A small square reminds me
To protect and love eternally
And the joy fills me for the moment,
But the past will last permanently in my heart.
Yet my small, secure, other world
Will remain hidden to others.

Louise Corner (13)
Sackville Community College

A POEM ABOUT WHAT IS SPECIAL TO ME

In this poem lies my life,
With happy thoughts and painful strife.
The beginning is a band of silver around my arm,
Welcoming me to the world with a silver charm.
Little steps, big strides in time,
Following the years I am about to climb,
Cutting through waves I have the power in my hand,
An image of my special world, symbolising time as sand.
Calling me softly, a voice from the past,
His loving way, he'll always last.
Like a lingering candle, burning all these years,
Overpowering my troubles, banishing my fears.
Moving on, I find my written obsession,
My whole life in one book, expressing emotion and aggression,
Words that will never fade, bringing warmth to my heart.
My musical passion is notes from the start,
Wheels that take me to no fixed destination.
With the wind in my hair, I feel my elevation,
Tranquillity is round my neck, bringing a sparkle to my eye,
The end is the fluffy ghost that will never die.

Katharine Gadsden (13)
Sackville Community College

MY LIFE

The closest to me wherever I may go,
A frustrating sound which takes me
To a life-long friend, the closest to my heart.

Memories which will always make me smile,
Easing the pain of loss and love.
A distraction for when things get too much,
Not forgetting my friend who is always there.

A ring of silver, a symbol of love and care,
But can no longer be worn, and
A band around my neck
Reminding me never to forget.

The beginning of my friendships and trying
To prepare us for success, the days of no stress or worries,
When my precious present and my security
Comfort me on my way.

And when it's time for privacy,
I return to my place of comfort and safety.

Leanne Blackwell (14)
Sackville Community College

MY LIFE IN A SHOE BOX

A silent reminder of good times past,
Still fresh in my mind and there to last.
My spherical hobby and love of life,
A passionate sport, but source of strife.
The key too well travelled, metallic companion,
From mile to mile, to old from young.
That paper memory of a golden day out,
A happy occasion to cheer and shout.
My furry friend who will never let me down,
Who is always there waiting when I come home with a frown.
The entrance to comfort, to warmth, to security,
My place, my cat, my sleep, my privacy.
A glossy memory of how I want to recall
Now fallen away, it doesn't seem that way at all.
Precious words saved as a recollection of before
And although I've aged somewhat,
I still enjoy reading them more and more.
A golden memory of a golden man with a story,
No wheels could stop him from achieving his glory.
And with this time he is all but gone,
While my life in a shoe box has just begun.

Adam Simpson (14)
Sackville Community College

MY POEM

The time upon my wrist
Leads me through the day.
Important information
I can hear from my pocket every day.
It's fun, I play games, I can talk to my friends,
I listen to it, I hear it loud and clear,
The only way I can relax.
A face I look at, but cannot talk to,
It reminds me of a fun time I had.
I use it to cut my way through life,
Like a fold-up tool.
It guides me though the night,
I see it very bright.
I can use it for games,
I can use it to see,
I use it for information,
I use it for fun.
You can use it wherever you are.
It makes everything dark,
It protects me from the lights.
I use it for times I don't want to forget, and faces.
I can look at it for when they're not here.

Ben Marshall (13)
Sackville Community College

MY WORLD

A special comforter, protecting from confusion,
Familiar. Relief as it returns.
Unique words unlock the delicate, desperate past,
Looking forward, rarely back.
A picture, no more, of an uncertain relationship,
A friend gone, but never to be forgotten,
Life goes on.
Problems blamed are not solved,
They just lengthen the suffering,
A prize mirrors the weak struggle for life, a lost battle,
Messages scribbled joyfully,
The end as a new door opens,
Amazing companions to forever be with me,
Tears to be defeated by laughter.
A frozen image. Life showing strength and love,
The power to grieve
Becomes the power to forgive and forget.
My lifeline
Provides me with private communication
As I stumble through life.
Mistakes are learnt, grudges withheld
Independence, a giant step forward
Towards another route down life's path.

Vicky Sellars (13)
Sackville Community College

CHILDHOOD

An orange-trunked comfort, her first words name,
By a chubby-cheeked innocence, who pointed her toes and tucked in
her tail.
Affection withheld, improvised by someone who wants it returned,
But will find out later it was always there.
Playtime chum, whose token is secretly treasured,
To remind her of a time when all was carefree.
In her memory, she still hears them meow.
Her blonde-haired role model,
Now matted and tu-tu lost,
No longer dances in hery imagination.
Whereas her light,
From one whose will soon grow dim,
Refracts colour and happiness in her room, her space,
Noon after noon after noon.
Notes that flow easily in practice stumble and fault,
But are rewarded by a piece of paper and generous parents.
Which from one sprang her interest of sound and how it is captured.
And now she is growing up,
With an artificial smile that brought man-made confidence.
Colours, shapes, stars and twinkles,
To attract attention,
To give identity,
To be individual -
Just like everyone else.

Ruth Bruce (14)
Sackville Community College

LIFE IN A SHOE BOX

The end of an era that will never feel or be the same again,
Strange new beginnings and weird scenarios that will
Influence my life forever.
Tension builds and secrets unravel which
Change my opinions of the people I love.
My tear-catcher always waiting in my sanctuary,
Free from the people I need to distance myself from
To keep my sanity, the place I can be myself
And not have to hide my feelings.
Bouncing ball of fluff and happiness that takes away the bad.
Reassuring signs of love that are more precious than stones.
A key to all my childhood memories, good and bad,
Soon to have new memories in place of mine,
The walls soon to hear a new story.

Lauren Bradford (14)
Sackville Community College

OCEAN OF LOVE

My tiny feet patter to the Nutcracker Suite,
Tinkling the ivories to play a tune,
Familiar faces comfort me,
When my heart is sad for my long lost friend.
A tag for everyone to know me by name,
And a sweet kiss from my bear, the first of many.
Sleeping Beauty pricks her finger
Over and over again.
A precious gift from past loved ones.
A little French book, alone on the shelf,
Never to be read by anyone else,
Maybe a key to a secret
In a diary I keep.

Cathy Lippert (13)
Sackville Community College

PAST AND PRESENT

A face no longer with us, but still in memory,
A precious life not to be wasted that is cherished every day,
Flying high, a rainbow of colour gliding by,
A companion loved, missed and need,
One short life, died in peace,
Memories of the way life once was,
Baby's steps turn into baby's crawls,
Loved ones behind you every step of your life,
One loved creature bringing infants to this world,
Memories of the way life once was,
A silver band wrapped round a young one's wrist,
A treasure to keep forever.
Memories of the way life once was.

Lucy Stiller (13)
Sackville Community College

A BOX OF MY PAST

As those six faces look over me,
I still remember them.
I used to have a lot of fun,
And I still hear the tunes.
I never had much of it but
The little amount I had was used well.
I get in touch with my family
Everywhere and at every time.
I took small steps, but big strides,
My need for speed and power.
It got me through some tough times.
It was my entrance to my home.
I could keep time.

Jon Batters (13)
Sackville Community College

ME

My two close friends, gone somewhere else now,
But still remembered by many pictures.
Shining, gleaming, white and black fur,
Groomed to perfection, and the coloured rope
That used to take you across green fields
And through dark, green forests.
In your place comes new sharp claws,
Loved just as much, but you are not forgotten,
These claws attack the still ball of fluff, but never hurt it.
And another soft object, held close for comfort.
A brilliant sparkle as the band hits the light,
Next to it my sight for an underwater world.
Memories of happy times and people close,
Communicating block for when I am alone with
My silver pass, my gateway to shelter and safety.

Louise Read (15)
Sackville Community College

MEMORIES

The past is caught in still images
Contained in a dust-covered book
And a shirt with many names.
My memories on a shelf
Remind me of a moment
That can never be captured again,
As my ticket to life was given to my
By a strong influence who is drifting further away,
My only memory of him is a small cartridge
Of undeveloped fun and a holy drinking shrine.

Aidan Bramall (14)
Sackville Community College

MY LIFE IN A BOX

Years of practice with money spent
Buckets of adrenalin and serious injuries,
Dreams of fame shot down by reality
Lessons and perseverance improving me slowly,
Skills passed down from generations
Admired by man,
Heavy and mellow power in every word
Fearless in many ways
With electric paintings to prove it.
Fantastic after-death images from the beginning
For those who find a personality under cover
A long time together is likely,
Worn when possible held close to my heart
Bought by a creator worn by number one,
Wanting, eating, loving.
The ability used when needed,
Appreciated when the job is done.

Howard Stagg (15)
Sackville Community College

MY LIFE IN A POEM

The best team can always bring out the joy in me.
My reflection appears in a circle of gold.
Memories and faces may very soon fade away,
Final task, leaving childhood behind
And moving on to adulthood.
The devils remind me of the days gone,
A band of gold with memories to last.
Half-pipe is my life with sounds bursting out.
From older generations, I still remember the first gift I got.
Every time I see my family, the love will not be lost.

Shane Atkinson-Beney (13)
Sackville Community College

MY LIFE IN A SHOE BOX

A memory of important times,
Maybe some day to be seen again.
Someone I will always remember, even after death.
Although we weren't allowed to be close,
Our limited times were special.
Precious and dreamy days always close by.
A special childhood friend was always there
And best friend from the past
We were bound forever,
We jumped the moon and dodged stars,
We were never really close, but loved each other.
She and I have shared with the rest of Britain,
Generations to come will not see them.
The most important place, full of friends and family,
I will never lose this, whatever happens,
Treasured memories, my life.

Rebecca Jessop (14)
Sackville Community College

LIFE

A glimpse of my past clutched in my arms,
Stood still behind glass stands a painting of love.
A shiny gold circle hung round my neck.
Nose, eyes and ears in a sea of black fur.
Tick followed tock, followed tick, followed tock.
It may look plastic and fit in my hand
But in reality, it's grand and lives not just on land.
With these I shared good times and grew.
Hard and tiring work was upon me.
Tick followed tock, followed tick, followed tock.

Rachel Shram (13)
Sackville Community College

MY LIFE

We play together, innocently,
A bundle of joy to comfort me.
On the sight of my passion I can ride so free
To the distant tribe many miles away.
The patter of tiny feet all those years ago,
Like the sound of a voice, but not its own words.
A little circle ties him to me,
Though one day we will both cease,
What is between us goes on eternally.
Two small rings remind of the bond,
As lying together a new identity begins.
Together they lived, I loved them together,
Walking together, a source of happiness.
The gold like a leash moulded by loving hands,
Arriving at a momentous moment of my time.

Rosie Jonsson (13)
Sackville Community College

A POEM OF MY LIFE

Words are written to amuse me for hours,
A place to let me unwind and relax.
Words remain only in my memory,
Words from my old friends stay in the past,
Memories from the depth of the earth,
A ball of fur so soft and cuddly
Stays in my mind for a lifetime,
A gift from far away will stay with me,
A drawing always in my head.
Sounds echo from far away,
A picture to stay in my mind for eternity.

Katie Robson (13)
Sackville Community College

MEMORIES

An image of a friend, never forgotten,
A family holiday, captured in a moment,
Wonderful sounds in the form of lines,
The language of music.
A mirror of me, a decade ago,
Humorous pictures, humorous words,
A red rose on blue, the symbol at school.
Round and silver, spinning on for eternity,
An entrance to warmth in a small metal tool,
Communication through words or sounds.
Always warm, even in winter,
All of these held in my mind,
Never to be released.

Alex Ormrod (13)
Sackville Community College

MY POEM OF MY LIFE

A small band of Christ,
Pictures of memories past,
Miniature modelling to fill my time,
An achievement to be proud of.
The thrill of winning around my neck,
Advanced power in history in my hand,
Magical leaves unfold to enhance my imagination,
Small beginning with room to grow.
These pieces of paper opened a world of learning,
Small disc of history brought to the future.

Daniel Hemsley (13)
Sackville Community College

MY MEMORIES

A faithful companion, now only in memory,
A great player wearing the
Great red material with pride.
Flashes of gold and silver
Show my achievement.
A sphere-shaped piece of leather
Keeping me amused.
My way of communication
With my friends.
Great sounds available at the press of a button,
A splash of a tail in the water,
Telling me I'm not alone.
A picture in my mind,
With me always.

Zac Curtis (13)
Sackville Community College

LIFE MY WAY

The ticking assures I'm never late,
Lost in my own world,
Hearing only what I want.
The piece of silver which unlocks my life,
Sun, sea and sand,
Precious time spent on completing
Magic paper, influencing me.
The need for a sudden rush,
The ringing in my ear with keeps me in touch,
The gift I never leave.
Looking at life my way.

Sam Davis (13)
Sackville Community College

MY POEM

Saved with love for a rainy day,
A present from my previous abode,
A symbol of my beliefs from across the water,
A small memento from a big occasion,
One of which I will never forget.
A way to entertain, letting my fingers do the work,
My precious companion's favourite pastime.
And aid to poise
Streaking through the blue for a prize worth winning.
Those that matter to me, gathered together, framed.
A magical journey to an enchanted castle,
My life is like a maze.
Around every corner lies something different, new,
But some things I'd rather keep safely locked away in my memory,
So that I will never forget what they mean to me.

Philippa Pawsey (14)
Sackville Community College

MY LIFE

A face I see in my head, but not very well,
An electrical system keeping me amused,
A piece of silver I can remember winning,
Like it was yesterday.
A great piece of white material I wear as a symbol,
Gold I see in my memory,
A pet I loved that is no longer here.
Sounds for my ears no one can hear,
The way I communicate with my friends
When I'm away,
I remember my friends when I'm not with them.

Sean Daoud (13)
Sackville Community College

TREASURES

Present from a relation,
First award for my love and talent,
Certainly not the last,
Forgotten are the steps,
But the song still dances in my head,
Words of my happiest memory
Close to me I keep,
Chain of silver binds us together,
Forever and ever I pray,
Though not the king of gifts,
I look at this and think of her,
Friendship dearer
Than any jewels in a ring,
The small animal's home,
My love surrounds it,
Furry companion,
I know no life without
Little magical creatures,
My worries they do take,
Always.

Pauline Fallowell (14)
Sackville Community College

ANGELS

I'm an angel,
Who would have thought?
Tim Reimoser,
An angel,
Well here I am,
Working for God,
But to tell you the truth,
God is actually Rex the Runt.
Yeah, that's right.
People may think angels wear gowns,
I don't think so,
I started the trend of broken watches,
Jeans,
Nike Athletic T-shirts,
Baseball caps and,
Most importantly,
Instead of using boring old bows and arrows,
We use up-to-date love-machine sniper rifles,
And instead of flying souls to heaven,
We now pick them up in Ferraris.
Yeah,
An angel's life is a lot more than some people may think.

Timothy Reimoser (13)
The Littlehampton Community School

INDIVIDUALS

There is one school system,
Not educational,
More sociable,
It's all about groups,
Groups of people.
They look the same from afar,
But are a little different at heart.
There are popular kids, full of confidence and power
Inside a hard, nut shell.
Then there are outcasts, scared and alone,
The middle of every joke, the bottom of the scale.
Then there are 'boffs,' or so they say,
Clever and happy and brainy every day.
Also there are bullies, hard and frightening,
No one is safe from their mean, scary lightning.

Then there's me, an individual I like to think,
But the thing is, their different worlds are not so different
At the depth of their hearts.
They are all individuals, together and apart.
They all have a heart,
And emotions,
Someday the nutshell will break and
The individuals will emerge, alive and awake.

Elizabeth Skilton (13)
The Littlehampton Community School

JERRYS

An ocean of brown and red surrounds me
As I crawl across the bloodies wasteland.
Screams of injured men haunt me as I walk by,
Guilt fills inside me as the Jerrys' mangled bodies lie on the floor.
They call it no-man's-land,
Which is far from believable.
The trench is like stepping into a red bath,
Full of wasted men and what's left of them.
Rats don't help.
They bring disease and maggots.
The first snowflake falls,
Christmas! The carnage will soon end.
No, this will never end . . .

Joe Kite (11)
The Littlehampton Community School

COUNTING POEMS

Only one octopus called Ollie of Octoland oddles around,
Two tiny toddlers try to teach tigers to talk,
Three thirsty thirteen year-olds think thunder's thrilling,
Four friendly foxes fighting for flying fish,
Five fierce Frenchmen furious in foreign forests,
Six strong, smarmy soccer substitutes swallow soggy,
                              scrambled sandwiches.
Seven Sallys snip some special spaniel's hair,
Eight eggs watch every episode of EastEnders and Emmerdale,
Nine ninny nannies natter nonsense,
Ten turtles trap two twittering terns,
Eleven English earwigs with earache eagerly eat Edam,
Twelve teenagers tiptoe to touch the toy train.

Laura Cruickshank (11)
The Rydon Community College

A RIGHT-ANGLED TRIANGLE

A
right-
angled
triangle
has a right-
angle surprise,
surprise like a
 shark's fin, a book
corner, or even half
a square. It has a straight
back and a box it never gets
back. It's 90° where two straight
lines meet, this is all a right-angled
triangle. Nobody notices it, but it's special.

Jenny Reynolds (11)
The Rydon Community College

A RIGHT-ANGLED TRIANGLE

A
right -
angled
triangle
is pointed
and it stands
up tall. It is like
a shark's fin sticking
out of the deep blue sea.
It is like a sharp sheet of ice.
It is a leader standing in front of troops.

Annie Wyeth (12)
The Rydon Community College

JOURNEY OF A DROPLET

I am a droplet in a cloud,
Now I am feeling heavy,
Now I am raining,
Down, down, down,
Into the spring.
In the big, bold mountains
I trickle now,
Along with the glistening, melting snow.
In the swaying stream,
I sway from side to side,
Swelling from a stream into a river.
I swell with the river,
Until I flood and lay desolate
In a mourning marsh.
The sun beating hard
Draws me and other droplets
To the shimmering sky.
We wait to see
Where the Nile will take us,
On our journey as droplets.

Charlotte West (10)
The Rydon Community College

A WINDY NIGHT

A windy night is brewing
Like a boiling kettle, waiting to bubble.
Can you hear the swishing, the swaying, the whistling,
Like a lady's long ball gown swishing across the swept floor?

The wind is howling,
Like a wolf trapped in an iron-barred cage.
The wind is speeding,
Like a car in a race at full speed round the bend.

But slowly, very slowly at first,
The wind starts to calm down
And before you know it, you can't hear
The swishing, the swaying, the whistling.

The howling is lost,
The speeding has stopped
And all you can hear is the soft breeze
In the still air, waiting to race again!

Emma West (12)
The Rydon Community College

THE SKY PAINTING

The sky is like a painting,
With orange bled into gold,
Inky-blue splattered with silver,
Purple mixed with pink.
The sky is like a story,
A glowing sun,
Gently moving cotton wool,
Replaced by a silver moon.
The sky is like a jewellery case,
Lined with deep blue velvet,
Bearing a diamond bracelet
And silver pendant.
The sky is like a painting,
With orange bled into gold,
Inky-blue splattered with silver,
Purple mixed with pink.
The sky is like a painting,
With orange bled into gold,
The sky is like a painting,
Secrets to be told.

Samantha Leogue (12)
The Rydon Community College

ARITHMETIC

Arithmetic is where numbers fly like leaves in the wind,
Arithmetic is where you have to work and work
And work until you get the right sum.
Arithmetic is seven, eight, a lovely fudge cake,
Or eight, nine climbing the vine.
Arithmetic is numbers calculating in your head
Until you get the right answer.
Arithmetic is where the answer is right and everything is nice,
Like a sunny afternoon at your favourite beach,
Paddling in your favourite pool.
Arithmetic is where the answer is wrong,
Like everything becoming extinct.
If you take a number and add it again and again and again,
It will get larger and bigger and huge!
Until you subtract it and make it small.
Arithmetic is where you have to divide and
Leave it in your head to remember.
If you have five slugs and your cat east two of them,
Where do the other slugs go?
Arithmetic is division, subtraction, addition and multiplication.
You have to learn it to understand it, you know!

Rosie Townsend (11)
The Rydon Community College

FORMULA 1 RACING

Companies running cars to be the best,
People get upset because they're behind the rest.

Sponsoring cars to make money,
Drivers trying to be funny.

Money is involved because of betting,
Faster, faster, cars are getting.

Steering cars is dangerous,
People getting furious.

People can *bash*,
So be careful you don't *crash!*

Leo Humphreys (12)
The Rydon Community College

THE HOT AND THE COOL

A melting dawn is opening,
Like a furious rushing river,
On trees and roads and hills and all
That can no longer feel.
But the spider is in his shady web,
Like a baby in a cradle.
But the bird is in his nest,
Like the milk in the fridge.
But the lioness is in her old cave,
Like an ice cream in the freezer.
But the badger is in his shady sett,
Like a lady under a parasol.

A nice hot morning is breaking,
Like an oven, sweltering hot
On the shiny railway train,
Of the streaming morning.
But the rabbit is in his burrow,
Like a horse in a shady stable.
But the fish is in his pond,
Like the child in the swimming pool.
But the pig is in his cool pig sty,
Like a child reading in the shade.

Charlotte Bristow (12)
The Rydon Community College

A RIGHT-ANGLED TRIANGLE

A
right-
angled
triangle
is always
tall and very
slim, with a box
in one corner. I
wonder what's in it?
It's like the corner of
a table, the corner of a
sign on the mast of a boat,
at the top of a shelf on the back
of a plane and rockets as well. Right-
angled triangles are everywhere. As tall
as a shark's fin sticking out of the water.

Christine Eales (11)
The Rydon Community College

I LIVE IN THE COUNTRY

I live in the country,
It's not all it's cracked up to be.
Yeah, I s'pose it's fun to be wild, reckless and free,
But I dream of the city lights, the rumble of the traffic.
People who complain about it say, 'You live in paradise.'
They *make me sick!*
At least they find friends close, they don't have to live in fear.
At least the hunter isn't there to make the rabbit shed a tear,
But I live in the country.
It's not all it's cracked up to be.

Faye Lord (12)
The Rydon Community College

A RIGHT-ANGLED TRIANGLE IS . . .

A
right-
angled
triangle is
like a mirror
staring back at
you in your reflection.

A right-angled triangle
is like rows of sweets
waiting to be eaten
by children
who have
been
good
!

Emma I'Anson (12)
The Rydon Community College

LIFE

Groovy is when life is fun,
Painful is when life is taken,
Hope to live in peace,
Wish to live forever,
Hard life is frustrating and sad,
Useful is when your life is helpful,
Life is just one big *war!*

Ryan Geal 12)
The Rydon Community College

175

GOD

It is the music in our souls,
The dancer in the flame,
The controller of time,
The maker of the stars,
The artist's paintbrush,
The words in a book,
The colour of our eyes, our skin and our hair,
The beauty in nature,
The water in a raindrop,
The sound from our mouths.

It does not judge, nor does it hurt,
It is the maker, the giver of life,
It takes no form or shape,
It is just there, perfect, whole.
It is God.

Lucy Rowan (12)
The Rydon Community College

IT IS A NIGHT IN NOVEMBER

It is a night in November,
It is a dark, gloomy, cold night in November.
I am walking fast, sad, cold, creeping,
Softly through the avenue of trees.
I stop to listen to the sound of leaves falling off trees
Onto the ground, feeling sad, the leaves
Rustle in the wind and the trees,
As still as a rock sitting on a patch of green grass,
As straight as a plank.

Luke Cripps (12)
The Rydon Community College

A NOVEMBER NIGHT

It is a night in November,
I am walking briskly, hurriedly, steadily,
Through an avenue of tall trees.
Feeling slightly depressed, I stop to listen
To the sound of rotting leaves
Falling off moss-filled trees.
It reminds me of bombs falling in a war,
Which is now the wind, and settling
On the ground, waiting for the slightest
Movement to trigger them off.
I look around. I see the leaves and realise
I'm in a minefield of imagination.

Maisie Crook (12)
The Rydon Community College

IT IS A NIGHT IN NOVEMBER

It is a night in November,
It is a dark, cold, creepy night,
In November.

I am walking slowly, scared, full of fear,
Through an avenue of long, skinny trees.

I stop to listen to the sound of leaves
Falling to the ground,
Feeling sad, like somebody has died.

It is a night in November.

Ben Maton (13)
The Rydon Community College

TERRORISTS

The human form of evil,
The type of people you don't want to know.
People who plot and plan
To destroy the world and cause havoc.
People who get pleasure
From causing pain and despair to innocent people.
People who should be locked up in prison,
For simply having no heart, or any sense of compassion.
They're people who've been taught
To throw away their own feelings, just to get revenge.
They don't have a caring bone in their body.
They're doing what they think is right, but deep down,
They know it's wrong.

Emma James (13)
The Rydon Community College

AMERICAN ATTACK

Terrorists are destroying this beautiful place,
It's hard to believe the terror on the face.
Pentagon and Trade Centre are not any more,
If only the future came quicker when we walk through that door.
I feel sorry for those people out there,
If only we could help, if only it was fair.
English and Americans, we will all fight back,
Against this disastrous attack!

Emma Tappenden (12)
The Rydon Community College

THE STORM AT NIGHT

A flash of lightning lights up the night sky,
Like a light bulb turning on and off,
Rumbles of thunder everywhere,
Like chairs and tables being moved upstairs.
But the children just look and listen,
Like a cat waiting for its dinner,
While the animals are trying to get some sleep,
Like mums and dads looking after a baby,
Like a tiger hunting for its prey
And the rain beats hard on the rooftop,
Like a giant knocking on the door.

Robyn Hyde (12)
The Rydon Community College

ACTIVE WATERS

A thick, slimy mess
Sitting on top of a smelly, untouched swamp,
With flies gathering on its muddy pile of reeds around its bank.

Huge, fresh, pure white waterfalls
Plunging down to a bubbling, fast-flowing rapid,
Crashing into wet slippery rocks to the pools below them.

A splattering, splashing, powerfully pounding wave
Winding quickly through the blue river as every drop changes
Itself into a mini-wave, leading on to enter the huge, gigantic ocean.

Jessica Read (10)
The Rydon Community College

A JOURNEY AS A SNOWFLAKE

Tops of mountains are waiting,
With dips between each of them,
Waiting,
Waiting for snowflakes.
At last they come, swirling,
Swiftly round and round with a gentle first touch to the ground,
Gradually into a pile of snow the snowflakes form,
With time it turns into water,
Pure water that trickles down the mountain top
Into a wild river of rapids,
With waves lapping each other,
Weaving through one another,
Then past the brook of bubbles,
Which overflows night and day on the way,
Cascading cataracts and lakes with live sounds of bubbles,
Which stand out the most of all the sounds,
Then after that there is the suspicious,
Surprising swamp, with a slow moving current,
Which makes it scary for some,
But the water keeps flowing, snaking down the mountain,
Getting close, closer to the ocean, falling down waterfalls
Into deep water, which falls into deeper water and comes back
To the surface, still overlapping one another.
The land now is flatter and now with a gentle current,
And on the banks, birds of all kinds and different sorts of animals,
But look now, the ocean blue, blue as anything
And now the journey to the sea has ended,
And this journey as a snowflake or raindrop will happen
Again and again.

Amy Rosoman (10)
The Rydon Community College

WHY DO I HAVE TO MOVE?

Why do I have to move
To a country so far away?
Why do I have to move
To a country of different ways?
Think of all the different things
That I'll leave behind,
My friends, family and people of all kinds.
My family I'll miss a lot,
Not only because of gifts,
But because of all the good times I've got
In memory, photos and scrapbooks.
My family has witness all kinds of times,
When I lost my first tooth
And learnt to ride my bike,
But then there were bad times,
Like falling off my brand new bike
And ripping the tyres
And getting my foot run over by a van.
So why do I have to move
To a country so far away?
Why do I have to move
To a country of different ways?
Think of all the different things
That I'll leave behind,
My friends, family and people of all kinds.
So why do I have to move
To a country so far away?
Maybe I'll find out some day.

Danielle Stagg (12)
The Rydon Community College

THE FINAL SHOOTOUT

The start of the final,
Determined to win,
You can feel the tension,
The crowd start to sing.

Half-way through,
The score is tied,
You know you're the best,
All anger has died.

Last twenty-four,
You're down by two,
You have the ball,
You're hit and you fall.

The foul is called,
You line up,
You try to think,
But trust your luck.

The first one falls,
The second one sinks,
The third one's launched
And nobody blinks.

It scores!
You win!
You are the best,
In that blue and red vest!

Matt Watson (13)
The Rydon Community College

NESUKA, QUEEN OF LEOPARDS

She basks out in the sun,
Her paws dangling on a branch above,
Her coat golden and sleek.

She is a strong hunter, is Nesuka,
And there she lays down to sleep.
As her tummy rumbles,
She purrs and pauses

And in brief seconds she has pounced and caught.
She eats quickly as out of the corner of one eye,
She sees a lion and quickly she sprints to a clear lake.

There she sees elephants squirting water,
Hippos bathing in the cool mud,
Fisher birds intently scanning for fish

And as she laps water onto her tongue,
She stares into the sunset.
She sees pinks merging with orange and blue,
A pure sparkling twilight.

Quickly, Nesuka jumps into a tree,
Turns and lays her head,
To dream a dream of days to come.

Rose Kearl (11)
The Rydon Community College